# THE CIVIL SERVICE

*Neil McNaughton*

*Series Editor: David Simpson*

Hodder & Stoughton

A MEMBE~

# DEDICATION

To my mother and father, who gave me my education.

# ACKNOWLEDGEMENTS

Thanks to Luke Hacker and Chris Loades for their work in the publishing of this book. The Publishers would like to thank "PA" Photos for permission to reproduce the photographs on pages 40 (Martine Keene), 46 (Michael Walter) and 68 (Stefan Rousseau). They would also like to thank the British Film Institute for permission to reproduce the photograph on page 35.

Orders: please contact Bookpoint Ltd, 39 Milton Park, Abingdon, Oxon OX14 4TD. Telephone: (44) 01235 400414, Fax: (44) 01235 400454. Lines are open from 9.00–6.00, Monday to Saturday, with a 24 hour message answering service. Email address: orders@bookpoint.co.uk

A catalogue record for this title is available from The British Library

ISBN 0 340 77458 4

First published 2000
Impression number  10  9  8  7  6  5  4  3  2  1
Year                      2005  2004  2003  2002  2001  2000

Copyright © 2000, Neil McNaughton

Cover photo from "PA" Photos, picture by Tony Harris

Typeset by Transet Limited, Coventry, England.
Printed in Great Britain for Hodder & Stoughton Educational, a division of Hodder Headline plc, 338 Euston Road, London NW1 3BH by Redwood Books, Trowbridge, Wilts.

# CONTENTS

# PREFACE

A/AS Level syllabuses in Government and Politics aim to develop knowledge and understanding of the political system of the UK. They cover its local, national and European Union dimensions, and include comparative studies of aspects of other political systems, in order to ensure an understanding of the distinctive nature of the British political system. The minimum requirements for comparative study are aspects of systems with a separation of powers, how other systems protect the rights of individuals and how other electoral systems work.

*Access to Politics* is a series of concise topic books which cover the syllabus requirements, providing students with the necessary resources to complete the course successfully.

*General advice on approaching exam questions*
To achieve high grades you need to demonstrate consistency. Clearly address all parts of a question, make good use of essay plans or notes, and plan your time to cover all the questions.

Make your answers stand out from the crowd by using contemporary material to illustrate them. You should read a quality newspaper and listen to or watch appropriate programmes on radio and television.

*Skills Advice*
You should comprehend, synthesise and interpret political information in a variety of forms:

- Analyse and evaluate political institutions, processes and behaviour, political arguments and explanations.
- Identify parallels, connections, similarities and differences between aspects of the political systems studied.
- Select and organise relevant material to construct arguments and explanations leading to reasoned conclusions.
- Communicate the arguments with relevance, clarity and coherence, using vocabulary appropriate to the study of Government and Politics.

David Simpson

# 1

# WHAT IS THE CIVIL SERVICE?

## Introduction

THE CIVIL SERVICE in Britain is perhaps the least understood part of the political system, yet it is of crucial importance to an understanding of how government works. Most students of politics will come to the subject with a generalised understanding of what civil servants do, but few have an intimate knowledge of the role and significance of the institution.

Many will also hold a considerable number of preconceptions about civil servants. The BBC comedy series 'Yes Minister' and 'Yes Prime Minister' from the 1980s presented a picture of powerful scheming officials enjoying themselves in a game of thwarting the plans and ambitions of elected ministers. Other popular images are of lazy, stuffy, essentially boring men in formal suits with petty minds and a lack of understanding of the real world. Such stereotypical characters seemed to have little purpose in life other than to eat up public expenditure and ensure that they enjoyed a trouble-free career with a generous pension at the end of it.

These images certainly contain elements of accuracy as well as a number of misunderstandings or superficial prejudices. Whatever the truth may have been in the past the civil service has changed dramatically in the last two decades of the twentieth century. The transformation from the traditional image of the service to the modernised institutions which exist today will be described later in this book. There will also follow, in Chapter 2, a precise definition of the civil service and of the officials which inhabit it.

Before we attempt this definition, it is important to take an overview of the governmental environment within which the civil service operates. This can be found in the preceding sections. There follows a brief description of how the civil service has developed since the mid-nineteenth century. For the purposes of contemporary study, the period after 1979 is by far the most relevant, but the developments which led up to that time are also useful to review. These are described in the section entitled 'The Development of the Civil Service' below. Finally in this introduction we will take an overview of the changing nature of the role of the British state. Greater detail will follow in later chapters.

# THE NATURE OF THE STATE AND GOVERNMENT

If we wish to understand the role and importance of the Civil Service in Britain it is important to understand the difference between the nature of 'state' and 'government'. The two words are often seen as interchangeable, but they do in reality refer to significantly different political functions. In strict constitutional terms the Civil Service is predominantly part of what we call the **state**, but political reality tells us that it (or at least the senior members of it) are effectively part of **government**. Once we know what the terms mean we can understand this apparent potential confusion.

## THE STATE

This is a collective term for all those institutions which are permanent and which administer the country as a whole. Being permanent they are expected to behave in a politically neutral way. They do come under the control of the elected government of the day and, as such, must obey their political masters, but this does not mean that parts of the state are expected to develop policies of their own. They *implement* policy, but do not *make* policy.

The Head of State is the reigning monarch and we certainly expect that the Queen does not become actively involved in politics. When speaking publicly she can neither make nor criticise the policies of the elected government. She sometimes refers to it as *my* government – for example when she opens Parliament annually and describes the legislative programme for the next twelve months – but in reality it is the people's government, not hers.

So what does the term 'Head of State' imply? There are a number of answers. Firstly it means that she represents all the citizens of the state in a non-political way. She is a **symbol** of our **unity** despite the political conflicts which may divide us. Secondly, she is in a position to take control of the state as a whole if there is a political crisis or emergency of some kind the elected politicians could not solve. If, for example, a government attempted to act outside the law she could theoretically step in on behalf of the citizens and dismiss such a government. Thirdly, she heads the permanent institutions of the state. This does not mean that she controls or manages them. Rather, it suggests that the ultimate allegiance of those who run the institutions of the state is to her.

Some examples will serve to illustrate:

- The police, judges, magistrates and all law officers are expected to serve the law. The law, in turn, though it has been developed through the centuries by successive governments, is the law of the Crown – the Monarch. The courts are the Queen's Courts in effect. She is symbolically present in every legal case. Indeed, in every court room the Queen's coat of arms can be seen to remind everyone of this fact.
- Members of the British Diplomatic Service who staff embassies and consulates abroad act in the name of the Queen. Foreign powers, after all, feel they are dealing for most of the time with the United Kingdom as a whole rather than its temporary government. As they are *Crown* servants there is some confidence that they represent Britain and not just her ministers.
- Civil Servants – the main subject of this book – are technically 'Servants of the Crown'. This expresses the idea that they are permanent and have a commitment to serve Britain *no matter which party happens to be in power at any time.*

We may now make a realistic list of the main institutions which are part of the state as it is defined here. These include:

- the Civil Service;
- the police and other law enforcement agencies;
- the Prison Service;
- the Diplomatic Service;
- the Intelligence Establishment;
- all public bodies not in the Civil Service such as quangos;
- public Corporations such as the BBC;
- the Armed Forces;
- the National Health Service.

This list, though not fully exhaustive, serves to demonstrate the principal aspects of the British state.

It is a moot point whether we should include parliament (both Commons and Lords) and members of the government of the day (i.e. ministers) as part of the state. Strictly speaking we should not. However, this might be misleading as government and parliament are effectively in political control of the institutions of the state. A way out of the dilemma is to suggest that they are *temporary* parts of the state. They can never truly claim to represent us all as a single, unified people as other parts of the state can, but they will claim to represent the broad national interest. Furthermore it is the government, not really the Queen, which speaks on behalf of Britain in dealings with foreign powers.

The state, then, is the permanent apparatus which keeps the country running, maintains order and security and seeks to retain national unity even as elected governments come and go or even become paralysed by political deadlock. The civil service is the administrative centre of this state. If government were to disappear it is the civil service, together with the forces of law, order and security, which would run the country. All that would be lacking would be the *political direction* which elected ministers and parliament can provide.

GOVERNMENT

As we have seen above, the term 'government' is not the same as the 'state'. The principal constituent of government is the hundred or so ministers who are summoned by the prime minister to take political control of the state. This seems relatively straightforward. However, we know that ministers are not alone in making policy. They are helped by specially hired advisers and – most importantly for the purposes of this book – by a select group of senior civil servants. We can, therefore, make a case for suggesting that government comprises not only elected ministers but those who advise them on policy.

This is not to say that senior civil servants are politicians. They are are not. Rather, they are neutral elements in the government who advise on policy formulation and on the best way of implementing policy, but who do not make policy. This theme will be further explored later in the book.

The principles outlined above also apply to devolved government in Scotland, Wales and – possibly in the future – to Northern Ireland. There the *British* state remains responsible for law, order, security and some aspects of administration, but these national regions have their own elected governments.

PARLIAMENT

As we have seen, the position of parliament in this scheme is somewhat ambiguous. It can be seen as part of the state in that it is a truly *national* institution which claims to represent the people as whole. The House of Commons, on the other hand, is temporary and is elected on strictly political grounds. A case could be made for suggesting that the House of Lords, an unelected and more enduring body, is a state institution, but it too is heavily influenced by political allegiances and so cannot be described as neutral.

Parliament is also not part of government. MPs and peers may influence some policies and it is true that ministers are all drawn from parliament, but it is not government. Its role is largely confined to overseeing and scrutinising the operation of both the state and government. Among other things parliament seeks to ensure that both are serving the national interest, are taking account of important minority interests and are giving good value for taxpayers' money.

So it is best to see parliament as sitting somewhere between the state and government. It is strictly part of neither, but plays a key role in controlling both of them on behalf of the people.

Diagram 1 below summarises the relationship between state, government and parliament.

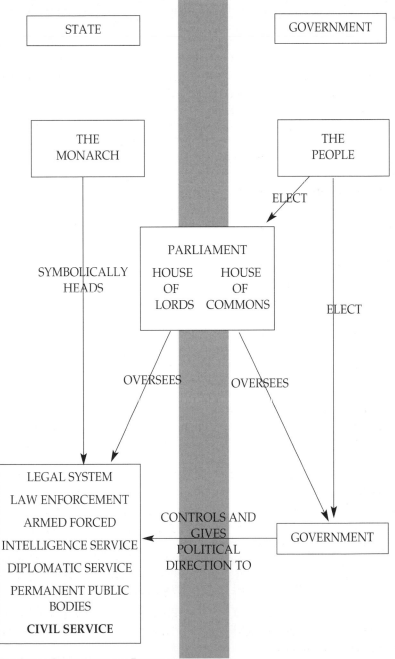

THE STATE, GOVERNMENT AND PARLIAMENT

# THE NATURE OF CENTRAL GOVERNMENT

Before about 1970 any picture of the structure of central government in Britain would have been relatively uncomplicated. It would have shown the prime minister and cabinet at the hub, with government departments reporting to them. Each department would have been headed by a minister and some subordinate junior ministers. Finally these departmental ministers would have been shown supported by a veritable army of civil servants, numbering over 700,000 in all. This is not to say that the relationships between these parts were not difficult to define, but the structure itself was certainly not confusing. By the end of the twentieth century, however, this was no longer the case.

A number of changes have taken place which add up to a more complex web of institutions and relationships. The civil service, which had remained fundamentally unchanged for a hundred years, did not escape the effects of these developments. The principal changes, described in detail in chapters 4 and 5, included the following:

- the role of the prime minister is acknowledged to have grown considerably;
- the Cabinet Office, a central civil service department, has grown in both size and importance. It now serves the political purposes of the prime minister and government as a whole, whereas in the past it was largely administrative in nature;
- ministers now employ a large number of personal advisers who are not civil servants;
- policy-making is a much more complex process than it used to be. A web of external 'think tanks', advisers, working parties, commissions, quangos and task forces now advise ministers on policy and have come to rival the influence of senior civil servants;
- the civil service itself has undergone a dramatic transformation in its structure. It is no longer a single, monolithic body, but has become instead a decentralised system of many agencies. These agencies have been separated from the senior civil service which is more closely involved in the policy-making part of government. This process will be described in more detail in chapter 4.
- The relationship between the civil service and the outside world is changing. The work of civil servants is far more open than it used to be to scrutiny by parliament, the media and the law courts. This situation is compounded by the introduction of a freedom of information act in 2000. The umbrella of secrecy which used to surround the civil service is gradually being lowered.

In order to clarify an increasingly complex picture, it is useful to think of the activity governing in terms of three processes:

1  **Policy-making**. This is the business of determining what direction the government should take, what new initiatives it will pursue, how it intends to solve new problems and how it will respond to new public demands. As an example we may take the Labour Government's plans to reform the welfare system at the end of the 1990s.

2  **Determining how to implement policy**. Deciding what to do is only the beginning of the process. The next stage is to decide how a new policy should be implemented. The principles of welfare reform may be established, but there are many important questions as to how the government's intentions can be successfully carried through.

3  **Implementation of Policy**. Once the *political* decisions (as described above) have been made, action must be taken. The changes must be made, the necessary administrative systems put in place and the new system must be operated effectively. Any new welfare programme will need new rules drawn up and imposed, staff recruited and/or trained and possibly a new management structure developed.

At each stage parts of the civil service must become involved. Diagram 2 on the following page illustrates these processes and indicates the role of the civil service at each one.

## THE DEVELOPMENT OF THE CIVIL SERVICE

### *1854–1968*

Before 1854 the civil service bore little resemblance to what we see today. It was, of course, much smaller. The scope of government was extremely limited, concentrating as it did upon the administration of a growing overseas empire, organising and financing the armed forces, collecting taxes, managing public buildings, controlling the issue and value of the currency, regulating limited aspects of industry, agriculture and foreign trade and undertaking public works, including transportation. Many of the functions we now ascribe to central government were then performed either by charities or by local authorities. These included education, welfare, health care and public utilities such as water and sewerage.

The limited number of civil servants were very different to the officials who inhabited Whitehall for much of the twentieth century. Most appointments were on the basis of nepotism – positions were given to a minister's relatives, friends and sons of friends. Similarly senior civil servants enjoyed their own powers of patronage and recruited juniors in their own image. Wealthy families with sons who had no great property, and did not enter the Church or the Army could always look to the civil service for a career which yielded a decent income without the need for serious work or stress. Those who hoped to make a fortune could enter the service of the Empire, especially in India, where they enjoyed opportunities for private enterprise and, in many cases, outright corruption.

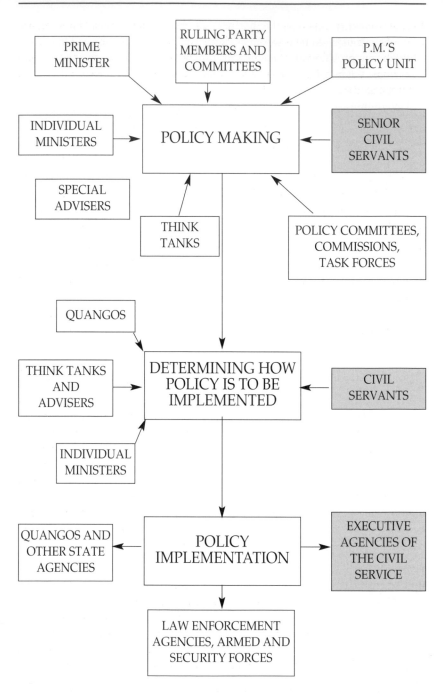

Needless to say members of the service came from a narrow social background, were often of dubious educational background and certainly did not owe their appointment or subsequent promotion to merit or hard work. There were exceptions, but most pre-1854 officials did relatively little work, were often corrupt and had a weak sense of public service.

In that year, however, the Northcote Trevelyan Report heralded the beginning of major changes. By the time it had been fully implemented in 1870 during the administration of William Gladstone, its reforms had fundamentally altered the nature of the service. The new senior civil service was now subjected to competitive entry (in practice by examination) and promotion was to be based on merit. The practice of appointment according to one's social contacts was largely ended. Above all, it became a professional, organised service with strict rules of conduct.

In truth the social make-up of the senior ranks of the civil service remained extremely narrow. It continued to be for many years exclusively male and was drawn from old boys of public schools, particularly graduates of Oxford and Cambridge. Yet it was now a professional organisation from which corruption and nepotism gradually disappeared. This was fortunate as the reforms coincided with the beginnings of a steady growth in the role of government and therefore the size of its administration.

As the size and scope of the state expanded senior civil servants steadily increased their political influence. There was less concern than there is today, that those who govern should be politically accountable. It was assumed that many of the best minds produced in Britain were members of the civil service and so they could be trusted with the administration of the country. Elected prime ministers and ministers came and went with varying degrees of political impact, but it was generally accepted that the activity of government was largely in the hands of the so-called administrative (i.e. senior) class of the civil service. For this reason senior officials came to be known as *mandarins*, a term which had historically been used to describe the appointed governors of imperial China. It was an apt description since, under most of the Emperors, the mandarins had also been recruited from those who were most successful in entrance examinations.

### 1968–79

By 1968, then, the civil service had become a huge organisation, numbering over 700,000 officials of all grades from the top mandarins down to lowly clerks and typists. It was known that the top few thousand officials – the administrative class – enjoyed great political influence. They were seen as virtually incorruptible, of extremely high ability and embodying a sense of public service which overrode the comings and goings of various governments.

The rewards for the maintenance of these qualities were impressive. They included great job security (it became virtually impossible to dismiss a civil servant for anything other than gross misconduct) decent if unspectacular salaries, a generous pension scheme and the knowledge that promotion to a reasonable level was assured provided serious mistakes could be avoided.

Serious doubts had begun to emerge in the 1960s that the British Civil Service was sufficiently effective. The 1968 Fulton report, commissioned by Prime Minister Harold Wilson articulated these concerns almost exactly a hundred years after the findings of the Northcote Trevelyan report had been implemented. Fulton praised the qualities of the civil service described above, but was also severe in its criticisms. Amongst its many serious conclusions were the following principal concerns:

- the service was amateurish in nature. Officials learned 'on the job' and were given little or no professional training;
- too many senior officials was 'generalists', that is they were experienced as administrators in general but had no technical knowledge which would be needed for the more specialised activities of government such as economics, science, planning or technology;
- the civil service lacked any sense of business practice. It did not consider, for example, value for money and did not monitor its own performance. These had become common practice in business and commerce, but not in public service;
- senior mandarins were poor at long-term, strategic thinking about policy. They tended to think in the short term and lacked a sense of progress and innovation.

Fulton's recommendations to eliminate these problems were largely ignored. This was partly owing to the civil service's own determination to resist change and partly the result of a lack of political will from three successively weak governments. Nevertheless Fulton was not forgotten.

In 1979 the election of a radical reformer to Number 10 – Margaret Thatcher – saw the Fulton Report taken off the shelf and dusted down. Its criticisms were added to a number of other concerns which had been identified and a new era of genuine reform was introduced. The post-1979 developments are described in detail in Chapter 4.

At the same time as the Fulton issues were being considered, worries began to grow that the civil service was exerting excessive political influence. A feature which had been of little concern until the 1960s suddenly came to the forefront of political comment. Most of this criticism came from politicians of the left such as Tony Benn and Barbara Castle. The Labour Governments of 1964–70 and 1974–79 had begun life with relatively radical political programmes. In both cases measures which were held dear by socialists were watered down or abandoned altogether. Some, though by no means all, of the politicians involved laid some of the blame on what they considered an ultra-cautious and obstructive civil service.

### *1979–Present*

Members of the Conservative government (not least its leader Margaret Thatcher) which came to power in 1979, also feared that the civil service was in no condition to undertake the extensive reforms it had in mind. Like the socialist doubters who had gone before, the new breed of Thatcherite Conservatives feared that the apparent conservatism (note the small 'c') of the civil service represented a barrier to their proposals.

As a result of such fears there began to develop a consensus that elected politicians should assert their political power. Whether or not the accusations of excessive political influence among the mandarins were justified, it became important for ministers to be seen to be in full control.

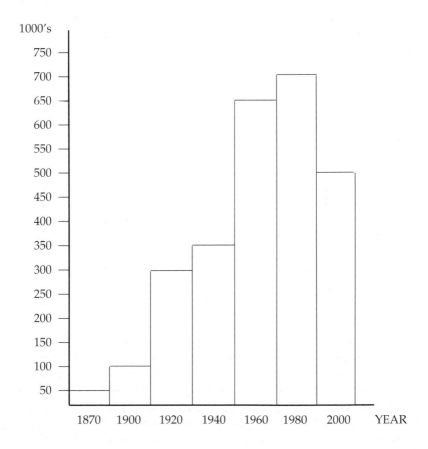

THE SIZE OF THE CIVIL SERVICE (APPROXIMATE FIGURES)

At the same time, Thatcher was determined both to reduce the size and scope of the state – in particular the civil service itself – and to change the way it operated in a fundamental way. Thatcher suspected that the civil service was oversized, inefficient and wasteful. It was, therefore, one of her first priorities to reform it. The nature of these changes are described fully in Chapter 4.

FROM PROVIDING TO ENABLING STATE

During the course of the twentieth century, and particularly since 1944, Britain saw a steady widening of the services which were provided by the state. These included:

- a comprehensive system of state education, providing free provision from the age of five through to degree level;
- a welfare state providing pensions, unemployment relief, support for poor families and a whole range of other benefits to those in need;
- the introduction of the National Health Service;
- the nationalisation of a number of great industries such as the railways, coal, steel, freight transport and telecommunications. This brought such activities under the overall control of government ministers;
- a range of regulatory activities were adopted by the state, for example concerning industrial relations, consumer protection and competition among private firms;
- it became accepted that the government should take an active role in control of the country's economy (so-called 'Keynesian' management).

It therefore came to be accepted that this state would **provide** a wide range of services and controls. The civil service was ready to take on this increased role. Two developments were then apparent. Firstly the civil service grew dramatically in size. Secondly civil servants came to see themselves as **managers** of this service provision as well as policy advisers.

Since 1979, however, the political climate has markedly changed. The three administrations which followed – those of Thatcher, Major and Blair, have all accepted that the private sector rather than state is better equipped to provide many of these services. Huge sections of the state, therefore, have changed their role from **providing** services to **enabling** the private or voluntary sectors to provide them. The enabling function involves such activities as determining who should provide services, ensuring quality and value for money, sometimes forming state-private sector partnerships, and generally protecting the public interest. Some of the main examples of this transfer of provision were:

- the privatisation of virtually all the great public corporations;
- relaxation of government control of the financial system;
- a considerably reduced role in active economic management;
- the privatisation of many local provisions such as housing, environmental services and road repairs.

These developments resulted in three principal changes in the nature of the civil service. Firstly it became much smaller as it was simply required to do less. Secondly its principal functions changed. It was recognised that senior civil servants need no longer be managers of services – that could be done by the private sector or by new institutions created within the civil service – but could instead concentrate more upon policy and policy implementation. Thirdly the growth in the importance of private sector services placed a greater burden of **regulation** upon the state. Thus many civil servants have changed their role from management to regulation. For example officials are no longer called upon to oversee the operation of great state industries, but are required to see that private industry does act in the broad public interest. This theme, of how the British state is changing and developing, is explored further in chapter 7.

# 2

# THE CIVIL SERVANTS

## WHO ARE THE CIVIL SERVANTS?

### THE CIVIL SERVICE DEFINED

THERE IS NO strict constitutional definition of the civil service or of civil servants. The Civil Service yearbook of 1999, produced by the Cabinet Office, describes a civil servant thus:

> *A CIVIL SERVANT is a servant of the Crown working in a civil capacity who is not: the holder of a political or judicial office; the holder of certain other offices in respect of whose tenure of office special provision has been made; a servant of the Crown in a personal capacity paid from the civil list.*

This is clearly not satisfactory and certainly tells us little about who they really are. Nevertheless, it *is* possible to construct a reasonably tight definition. To be called a civil servant one must be all or some of the following:

- employed directly by a central government department, or…
- employed by one of the executive agencies which come under the indirect control of a central government department, or…
- employed to work for the devolved governments of Scotland or Wales;
- employed in a manual or non-manual capacity either to help make policy, or to implement it or to run the administration of government;
- appointed but certainly **not** elected
- expected to act in a completely politically neutral manner, but…
- demonstrate utter loyalty, directly or indirectly, to the authority of one's masters – i.e. the ministers who control the civil service.

It is also worth noting some groups of public sector employees who do similar work, but who are **not** civil servants. These include:

- Local authority officers
- Members of the police and other law enforcement services
- Judges, magistrates and other officers of the law courts
- Private political advisers employed by ministers, MPs and political parties
- MPs, peers and ministers themselves, all of whom are either elected or are members of the legislature
- Non-elected officials employed by parliament
- Members of so-called quangos (see glossary) who are appointed by government but are not civil servants *unless* they have been seconded (temporarily transferred) from the civil service to such a quango.

There is a distinction between 'industrial' and 'non-industrial' civil servants. Industrial civil servants undertake manual work and we are not concerned with them in this book as they make no contribution to policy making or implementation.

## CIVIL SERVICE NUMBERS

In April 1998 there were 463,266 civil servants. This represents just under 2% of the total working population of the United Kingdom. To give some idea of the principal activities in which they are engaged the following 1998 figures are illuminating:

| Table 1: *Numbers of Civil Servants by department* | |
|---|---|
| ACTIVITY OR DEPARTMENT | TOTAL NUMBER |
| Department of Social Security | 87,193 |
| Ministry of Defence* | 75,851 |
| Inland Revenue (Tax) | 53,412 |
| Prison Service | 36,701 |
| Dept. for Education & Employment† | 33,117 |
| Customs and Excise | 23,400 |
| Home Office | 10,756 |
| Lord Chancellor's Dept. (Legal Services)** | 10,048 |
| Agriculture, Fisheries and Food | 9,613 |
| Diplomatic Service | 5,449 |
| Security and Intelligence | 4,896 |
| Cabinet Office (Central Government) | 1,947 |

*NOT SERVICE PERSONNEL. †NOT TEACHERS. **NOT JUDGES AND MAGISTRATES
SOURCE: CABINET OFFICE

Out of these totals, 364,163 civil servants are now employed by what are called 'Executive Agencies' (also known as Next Steps Agencies). These are described in detail in Chapter 4 below. The significance of being a civil servant in an agency rather than working directly within a government department is in one's terms of employment. In the agencies salaries vary a great deal; there are more incentives for those who are successful, but less job security for those who are not.

HOW TO BECOME A CIVIL SERVANT

Today (it was not always the case) one may enter the civil service at any of its various levels depending on qualifications, ability and experience. Most senior civil servants achieve their position by working their way up the hierarchy and by being promoted. However, the extent to which one may rise up through the service is heavily dependent upon one's educational background. It is, for example, almost impossible for an individual to enter the service as a lowly clerk or typist and work his way up to the most senior levels.

The top levels of the service – the so-called senior civil service – are almost entirely recruited from graduates with good degrees, very often from the more prestigious universities. Since the start of the 1980s an increasing number of senior positions in the executive agencies and the senior civil service are being filled by people who have enjoyed a career *outside* government, such as business executives, bankers, academics and the like. This new breed of civil servants obtain their position by applying for posts in the normal way and must often compete with existing civil servants who are working their way up through the ranks.

THE STRUCTURE OF THE CIVIL SERVICE

We should view structure in two directions. Firstly there are the various ranks into which the service is directed. These are as follows:

*Senior Civil Servants*
The top five ranks in the service. Each rank has a title. These are:

| Table 2: *The Senior Civil Service* | |
|---|---|
| LEVEL | TITLE |
| Grade 1 | Permanent Secretary |
| Grade 2 | Deputy Secretary |
| Grade 3 | Under-Secretary |
| Grade 4 | Varies |
| Grade 5 | Varies |

This group, comprising nearly 4,000 individuals, is the part of the civil service the rest of this book will be mainly concerned with. They are the 'mandarins' to which reference was made in Chapter 1. Most, though no longer all, have spent their whole career in the civil service, having entered as graduates in their early twenties.

These senior grades inhabit the great offices of Whitehall. They are in regular contact with their ministers and are intimately involved in the process of policy making and implementation.

### Specialists

Alongside the structure of the general or open civil service are a number of groups who have specific occupations and tasks. The largest group, known as the **Administration Group**, contains seven further groups from Senior Executive Officer down to administrative assistant. In other words, from quite senior service managers to humble clerks. A few of the most able may be ultimately promoted into the senior civil service, but these are the exception rather than the rule. We might call these officials specialised administrators. They manage services and the flow of information into the civil service as a whole.

Examples (not a complete list) of other specialist services are shown in the table below:

| Table 3: *Specialist groups within the Civil Service* | | |
|---|---|---|
| SERVICE | RANGE OF POSTS | FUNCTION |
| Science Group | Senior Scientific Officer down to Assistant Scientific Officer | Carrying out research projects for various departments. |
| Social Security Group | Local Officer grades | Assessing and delivering social security benefits |
| Economist Group | Senior to Junior Economic Assistants | Carrying out economic research, collecting information and disseminating to relevant sections. |
| Information Group | Senior to Assistant Information Officer | Gathering and publishing information to the media, the public and interested parties |

### Executive Agency Staff

As we shall see in Chapter 4, the new executive agencies which began to be formed after 1988 and which have been growing in number and significance ever since, are largely autonomous from the rest of the civil service. This means that each one is relatively free to develop its own structure, to recruit whomever it sees fit and to arrange its own systems of promotion.

They do have in common, however, the fact that they are headed by a **Chief Executive**. The Chief Executives are not in the same position as senior civil servants referred to above. Although they may be appointed by a minister with the help of his Permanent Secretary (i.e. his most senior civil servant), they are not involved in the policy making process. Their job is to ensure the effective and economical delivery of services such as the provision of welfare benefits, arrangements for road building programmes and the administration of driver and vehicle licensing.

The Chief Executives operate with a hierarchy of management and a veritable army of civil servants who carry out service provision. At the lower levels civil servants are graded according to the systems described above.

We will now return to the senior civil servants who make up the top five grades and examine who they are, where they come from and what is their role. We will then discuss the relationship which exists between senior officials and the elected ministers whom they serve.

THE CONSTITUTIONAL POSITION OF CIVIL SERVANTS

*The Nature of Bureaucracy*
Before looking at the constitutional status of specifically *British* civil servants, it will be helpful to consider the nature of **bureaucracy** in general. The term 'bureaucracy' literally means 'rule by officials', but this is slightly misleading. In any context, though government is the most common, a bureaucracy is the establishment of appointed officials whose role is to form the permanent organisation of an institution. They may not literally 'rule', but certainly make institutions work day-to-day and year-to-year. It is, however, accepted that they are servants of some higher authority. When we talk of a 'government bureaucracy' the higher authorities are government and parliament. There have been circumstances when bureaucracies in some countries have appeared to rule on their own account – in the old communist Soviet Union for example – but in mature democracies the central bureaucracy is expected to obey the elected government.

In Britain, therefore, the civil service forms the central bureaucracy. If we now consider some of the accepted principles of 'good bureaucracy', we can see how the British civil service compares to an ideal model. We can say that a good, effective bureaucracy in a democracy should demonstrate the following qualities:

- It should be politically neutral although it should be aware of the concept of national interest and be prepared to make this known to the elected government of the day.
- It should not be corrupt or corruptible, i.e. its members should not make decisions on the basis of personal or financial gain.

- It should treat individuals and organisations on an equal basis. In other words it should not discriminate irrationally against anyone who will be affected by its decisions.
- It should operate on the basis of strict rules of procedure and conduct so that citizens have a degree of certainty about how it will deal with them.
- A relatively modern principle is that a bureaucracy should be open to scrutiny and that its procedures and records should be available for inspection, provided the security of the country will not be endangered.
- Bureaucrats should be recruited and promoted on the basis of merit rather than personal favour.

Turning to the long established principles of the British central bureaucracy – its civil service – we can, in part at least, make some comparisons. It should, however, be noted that the importance of these principles extends only to those senior civil servants who are directly involved in policy development and implementation. Although they apply to more junior officials, they are of considerably less importance:

### Anonymity

This term does not mean that civil servants must behave like secret agents! (though, such operatives are, technically part of the civil service). What it does mean is that they must not reveal to the outside world – that is the world outside the immediate political community within which they work – the *precise* part they play in the political process. Their rank and status can be revealed and it is generally known in which section of a government department each one works. However, they cannot reveal the nature of the advice they have given, nor may they express any views on government policy in public. Whatever their private reservations on policy may be, they must remain private. Only ministers themselves should hear them.

On the rare occasions when civil servants do speak publicly – normally confined to testifying before select committees or MPs or to public enquiries on major issues – they are only permitted to explain known government policy (a system governed by the so-called *Osmotherly* Rules). Thus it is their precise *role* which is anonymous, not *themselves*.

### Neutrality

This is a more difficult concept in general. However, we can begin with a straightforward part of the rule. Civil Servants may not be politically active in any way. The most senior grades are certainly not allowed to be members of a party at all. Further down the ranks, passive membership may be tolerated, but there must be nothing more than payment of the subscription. Attending party committees or canvassing at elections is definitely forbidden.

There is, however, a more subtle meaning to neutrality. The difficulty arises because civil servants are, on the one hand expected to express no specific political views when giving advice, but on the other hand they must be faithful servants of the government in power. This suggests they should slavishly adhere to the ruling party line on all issues. The two ideas seem, at first sight, to conflict with each other. How are we to escape from the apparent paradox?

The best answer is to think of known government policy as a set of limits beyond which civil servants may not stray. *Within* these limits or parameters, however, they are free to express a range of alternative views. Indeed it is their duty to do so. We can therefore summarise the position as follows:

---

*Senior Civil Servants are required to give impartial, independent advice to ministers within the known parameters of official government policy.*

---

A problem does arise when there is no stated government policy on an issue; when, for example, a totally unforeseen problem arises. In strictly constitutional terms, the solutions should be developed within governmental circles – among ministers, party committees or private advisers – but it would be naive to believe that senior civil servants do not play a leading part in these circumstances. Here their neutrality should consist of pursuing what *they perceive* to be the national interest. It is certainly at such points that the political neutrality of senior officials is most severely tested.

Two examples may help us here:

- Transport policy is always a difficult area which requires extensive civil service involvement. The advice given must take account of public policy statements by ministers, perhaps favouring either private motoring or investment in public transport, so that civil servants should not pursue any line which contradicts the existing policy. Provided they do not, however, they are free to give whatever advice they think best.
- When an unforeseen foreign crisis emerges, such as the Kosovo war of 1999, there is no existing policy. Civil servants in the Foreign and Defence Department do not work under such strict limitations. They become free to suggest a wider range of options.

The principle of neutrality also suggests that civil servants should be able to serve different ministers and different ruling parties with equal faithfulness and integrity. The implications of this are explored in the third constitutional feature of the British civil service – permanence.

### Permanence

When a new government takes power in Britain, whether or not it is controlled by a different party to the last, all civil servants retain their posts. In this sense it is clear that they are permanent. Similarly, when an individual minister leaves his posts and is replaced, the new man or woman inherits all the civil servants in the department. This is in direct contrast to the situation in the United States, where as many as 4,000 officials may lose their jobs or be moved to different posts when a new President takes office.

Permanence also means that civil servants have very secure jobs. They cannot be removed on the whim of a minister, or because he does not like the advice the civil servant is giving, or because the minister's view of 'national interest' does not conform to that of the civil servant. The dismissal of a civil servant can only be justified, according to this principle, on the grounds of misconduct (such as financial corruption), incompetence or overt political bias.

The purpose of the permanence principle is twofold. Firstly it is designed to provide some continuity from one government to the next or when an individual ministerial office changes hands. The civil service can carry on the process of government seamlessly and without great upheaval while new governments or ministers settle in. Secondly it helps to preserve their political neutrality. If new civil servants were appointed each time a new government or minister took office, there is a danger that the new recruits would not be independent thinkers and might simply have been appointed on the basis of their known political views. The American system accepts this, but the British (and European) principle of neutrality cannot allow it.

If we look back at the principles of *bureaucracy* as described above we can see that the British civil service already conforms closely with them. When we add one further feature the two descriptions come even closer together. This is the code of conduct under which civil servants are expected to work. The principle is enshrined in the *Armstrong Memorandum* of 1985, a document published by the then Cabinet Secretary (and therefore most senior civil servant), Sir Robert Armstrong. This, and its 1997 updated version known as the *Civil Service Code*, deals with such issues as impartiality, loyalty and anonymity among civil servants. It provides a set of rules to which we can expect all civil servants to aspire, and against which we can judge them.

But having established that the *constitutional* position of the civil service stands up well to established principles, we must examine the extent to which the principles are carried out in practice. In other words, how well does *reality* stand up to scrutiny?

This question will be addressed briefly in the next section and in more depth in Chapter 3.

THE ROLE OF THE SENIOR CIVIL SERVICE

Most civil servants are engaged in either routine tasks or in the management of government services. The senior civil service, approximately 4,000 holders of the five senior ranks, however, are more closely involved in the political process. We must now examine the precise nature of their involvement. It is best concentrated into a number of functions:

## Decision-making

Government ministers are extremely busy people. They are called upon every day to make a bewildering variety and number of decisions. It is impossible for them to become personally involved in every one of those decisions. They must, in reality, reserve their scarce time for the most important and the most politically sensitive of those decisions. It is at this point that the crucial feature of trust enters the scene.

A minister must trust his senior officials to decide which decisions require his attention and which they can safely make themselves. This is a vital part of the process of government as *every decision is made in the name of the minister even if he has played no part in it*. He must, therefore, be sure firstly that the key ones are indeed referred to him and secondly that the decisions delegated to his senior civil servants are well made. Ultimately he may be called to account for them all.

What kind of decisions might be delegated in this way? Some examples will illustrate:

* the Home Secretary is frequently called upon to adjudicate on applications for citizenship, parole from prison, asylum requests and matters concerning the conduct of the police;
* the Board of Trade must decide whether to grant export licences for sensitive categories of goods and make final decisions on whether to allow large company take-overs and mergers;
* the Environment Secretary receives large numbers of applications and appeals concerning the granting of planning permission for large scale building developments;
* education ministers must make final decisions on whether schools may change their status, on matters concerning public examinations and university provision.

This small snapshot of the day-to-day work of government departments demonstrates the wide range of duties which officials must fulfil. In each case they must decide what needs to be brought to the minister's attention. If they decide to act themselves they must take into account the possibility of a challenge in the courts through the process of judicial review, criticism from an individual MP or a parliamentary committee, or adverse publicity from the media. In every case it is the minister in whose name the decision is made who must ultimately take responsibility. This creates an onerous burden on the civil servant. He must act with care, skill, rigour and integrity. In the next section of this chapter, which deals with the relationship between ministers and civil servants, we will see some weakening of the doctrine of ministerial responsibility, but it is still true that civil servants have to take into account the sensitive position of their political bosses when making difficult decisions.

### Dealing with the European Union

To an increasing extent government departments are having to deal with the realities of European Union membership. To match the growth in the importance of Europe a growing number of senior civil servants are being assigned specifically to European duties. Here they must gather information and brief their ministers on the multitude of proposals which pass through the European Commission and the Council of Ministers where final decisions are made.

This role largely consists of identifying the areas with which a minister should become involved, developing negotiating positions, explaining the attitude of the ministers from other member countries and recommending courses of action. In many cases much of the detailed negotiation between member states is carried out by these senior civil servants and their European counterparts. By the time ministers meet to make final decisions, most of the problems should have been ironed out. All that are left are the big questions of policy and choices between the various options available.

Those departments which deal frequently with Europe, such as the Board of Trade, Agriculture and Fisheries, the Treasury and the Department of the Environment have now developed special units of civil servants whose specific task is to deal with Brussels and other member states. We may hear little of their work, but to an increasing extent more and more of the activities of government fall within this category.

### Policy Advice

The doctrine of neutrality, as described above, appears at first sight to limit quite severely the scope for civil service involvement in policy development. But, this may be misleading. The role of the civil service is surprisingly extensive.

It is certainly true that senior civil servants are not expected to develop completely new policy. This is the task of party leaders. It is, indeed, explicitly stated in the *Questions of Procedure for Ministers*, issued to every new government minister, that civil servants *must not* be used in party policy making. But, where policy already exists, civil servants certainly are called upon to help decide *how* to implement policy, to sort out the *details* of policy and to help form policy under unforeseen circumstances. In many cases the whole success or failure of policy depends upon such considerations. It should also be understood that civil servants will be called upon to advise on whether ruling party policy is practicable, on the timing of its implementation, and the best way of presenting it to the media, the public and to parliament. Thus, civil servants are at the centre of the political process.

In many cases ministers recognise the need for consultation before important political decisions are made. The civil servants will normally arrange this. They will decide on the formation of committees, publication of discussion documents, meetings with interest groups and MPs and any legal requirements which are needed to legitimise a decision. Once all these arrangements have been put in place, their administration must be handled and the results relayed to the minister. Once again this must be in a clear, condensed form.

The most common procedure, after all the consultations are complete, is for civil servants to identify the key decisions which have to be made. They must also prepare a series of possible options, condense the information down sufficiently for ministers to be able to digest the information, make technical detail understandable and explain the various advantages and disadvantages of each of the options presented. Once again we must remind ourselves of ministers' busy schedules. The officials must bring policy decisions down to a form which can facilitate a speedy, but informed conclusion.

### Policy Implementation
Once a decision has been made it must be implemented. Here again the civil service takes over. A whole series of problems must be overcome. Some examples of this are as follows:

- How much will it cost and how is it to be funded?
- If it needs parliamentary approval, arrangements must be made for debate and consultation.
- Any legislation must be drafted. The wording of acts of parliament and other legal documents must be clear, must not conflict with any existing law (including today European Law), and must be capable of standing up to scrutiny by the courts. Every eventuality should be catered for in legislation to avoid future confusion and, in extreme cases, failure of the policy altogether.
- What institutions, if any, need to be set up? If they do, arrangements must be made for their establishment.
- How is policy to be presented? This key theme has become so important in modern times that it must be treated separately.

### Policy Presentation
At first sight this role would seem relatively innocuous and non-political. Indeed, until he 1960s this was the case. However, it has become increasingly complex and controversial.

The traditional tasks of civil servants cause little difficulty. These involve writing speeches for ministers, advising them on answering parliamentary questions from MPs and peers, preparing press releases, consultation papers, and briefings for ministers presenting a case to their cabinet colleagues. It is understood by all that these are valid activities and do not threaten the neutrality of civil servants.

The modern era, however, has seen a veritable explosion in the need for government departments to give out both information and to justify the policies they are adopting. Here, the manner in which policy is presented, especially to the media, has become a political issue in itself. At its most intense the issue of presentation has also become interwoven with the internal politics of the parties. Thus, when civil servants are asked to handle policy presentation to the media and *within* parties, they are in danger of losing their neutrality. For this reason, ministers have increasingly resorted to the use of private advisers who are *not* civil servants, and therefore not bound by the rules of neutrality, to present their case for a particular political viewpoint. These are the so-called *spin doctors* who have become so much a feature of modern politics.

In the next section this, together with a number of other issues concerning the relationship between civil servants and ministers, will be considered further.

## MINISTERS AND CIVIL SERVANTS

An article in the *Times* newspaper in 1977 presented the relationship between ministers and their officials in plain terms:

---

*The constitutional position is both crystal clear and entirely sufficient. Officials propose, Ministers dispose [i.e. decide], Officials execute.*

---

This presents a picture of a master-servant relationship where roles are clearly defined and where there is little controversy. The *Times* view was that it was civil servants who choose the options, ministers who decide between the options and then civil servants who ensure the decision is put into practice. Terence Heiser has expressed the relationship more colourfully by recalling the theme of the song about the *Vicar of Bray*:

---

*And thus is the law I will maintain unto my dying day, Sir,*
*That whatever king may reign, I will be the Vicar of Bray, Sir*

(quoted in D. Richards, *The Civil Service under the Conservatives*, Sussex Academic Press, 1997)

---

The *Vicar of Bray* also boasted that he was able to change his preaching depending on which king was on the throne, therefore preserving his position.

Much of the *Times* view and the words of the *Vicar of Bray* remain true. The civil service does adapt to new masters every so often and it remains true that ministers reserve the right to make final decisions. Despite fears expressed by radical ministers (such as Richard Crossman in the 1960s, Tony Benn in the 1970s and Margaret Thatcher in the 1980s) that the loyalty and co-operation of the civil service could not be guaranteed, there is much evidence to suggest that most civil servants have proved themselves both adaptable and subservient.

The arguments that civil servants do indeed wield considerable political influence and even power will be further considered in Chapter 3. However, at this stage we can be sure that the official position does, as the *Times* suggests. remain largely true. An area of undoubted change, however, concerns the nature of political accountability.

It used to be clearly the case that government ministers were expected to accept responsibility for *everything* done by their civil servants, whether or not they were directly involved in decisions made by them. The doctrine of **individual ministerial responsibility**, which covers this circumstance, could even extend to the resignation of the minister in extreme cases. It was certainly a valid principle up to 1983 when Lord Carrington, the Foreign Secretary, resigned over the failure of his officials to warn the government of the impending invasion of the Falkland Islands by Argentine forces. Carrington himself claimed that he had not been informed and so could not have taken preventive action. Nevertheless he accepted responsibility and paid the full price.

Thereafter, however, the principle has been steadily weakened. A number of cases have occurred when serious government errors did not result in ministerial resignation. The most notorious example emerged when the **Scott Inquiry** in 1993 revealed a catalogue of confusion, misleading of parliament and secret changes of policy concerning the control of the supply of arms and equipment to Saddam Hussein's regime in Iraq. Both ministers and civil servants were implicated in the scandal and were severely criticised by Scott. William Waldegrave and Sir Nicholas Lyell, the two ministers most severely censured, refused to resign and blamed civil servants for errors revealed by the inquiry.

If the aftermatch of Scott appeared to destroy the principle of individual ministerial responsibility, the behaviour of Home Secretary Michael Howard came to change it irrevocably. By 1995 the state of many of Britain's prisons, for which the Home Office under Howard was responsible, was seen as critical. There were frequent escapes, drug problems and even weapons discovered. Under growing political pressure Howard dismissed the senior official who headed the Prison Service, Derek Lewis. His argument was that the faults were 'operational' matters, not 'policy'. Thus he was not prepared to make himself responsible. In doing so he threatened not only the doctrine of ministerial responsibility, but also the status of senior civil servants.

The doctrine of individual ministerial responsibility served to underpin all three constitutional principles of the civil service. It safeguarded anonymity in that the precise role of a civil servant could be kept secret provided his minister was willing to take public responsibility for his actions. It could also take the pressure off civil servants where criticism was being levelled at the work of a department. Neutrality was similarly protected in that, if a civil servant could not be held responsible for their actions, it would be difficult to put political pressure on them to act in a certain way. Finally, permanence was most under threat. If civil servants are liable for dismissal (as Derek Lewis found) when criticism is made, they will lose job security and so may feel less free to give independent advice.

So, the erosion of ministerial responsibility has fundamentally changed the civil servant-minister relationship. It now appears that, if a decision can be attributed to an individual official, and if the minister can successfully claim that he played no part in the decision, the civil servant himself becomes publicly responsible. Only when a matter of policy specifically made by a minister is concerned, will responsibility lie with that minister. On the one hand this may, in the long run, prove to be a useful discipline on civil servants who have been protected in the past. On the other hand, by undermining their independence and security, it may jeopardise the quality of the service they give to ministers. Further details on this aspect of government can be seen in another book in this series, *UK Government and Politics in Context*, by David Simpson (see pages 60–72).

## WHO ARE THE MANDARINS?

### *Why is the composition of the civil service important?*
The nature of the people who fill the senior posts in the civil service is only important to students of politics if these individuals enjoy genuine influence in the processes of decision making and implementation. If they do not enjoy power or influence it becomes merely an academic question. This issue is considered in some depth in the next chapter, but at this stage we will assume that the senior civil service *does* have some influence.

It can be argued that the political role of civil servants may be influenced by the kind of people they are. What is their social and educational background? Are they predominantly men or women? Are they all middle aged, grey figures who have all graduated from public schools and Oxbridge? The answers to there and similar enquiries may give clues as to whether they are likely to be conservative (small 'c') in their thinking, whether they will tend to favour the interests of the middle and upper classes in policy considerations and whether they will be happier working with governments of the political left or right. It may also tell us something about their actual ability. Are they recruited and promoted purely on merit or on the basis of a favourable social upbringing? We may also legitimately ask whether their background is sufficiently varied for them to be able to bring wide experience to the advice they give and the work they do.

Three important perspectives on the make-up of the senior civil service have been particularly critical and demonstrate various aspects of this feature:

- The **Fulton Report** of 1968 suggested that a number of problems had resulted in a lack of effectiveness in the civil service. It suggested that too many senior officials came from a narrow social background – (largely traditional public schools and Oxbridge), had little or no experience of any other world than that of the civil service itself and that too few of them had any specialised knowledge of the fields in which they were working. The Fulton Committee and the prime minister who had appointed them – Harold Wilson – came to the conclusion that the traditional make up of the service would not be able to modernise Britain in the face of technological advance and intensifying economic competition from abroad. Though much progress has been made to reform systems of recruitment, the problem remains in place thirty years later.

- **Peter Hennessy**, in his definitive work, *Whitehall*, argues that the type of civil servants which Britain employs have left her ill-equipped to deal with her problems. He accuses many senior officials of seeking consensus instead of radical solutions, of thinking of short term solutions at the expense of long term strategy and of lacking the technical knowledge to support their undoubted administrative skills. Hennessy accepts that the civil service has many good qualities, but blames recruitment and promotion policy for many of its failings. He quotes Thomas Balogh to support his view:

> *[Britain is saddled] with an entrenched administrative class of non-specialist dabblers, renewed, generation after generation, by a recruitment process favouring the smooth extrovert conformist with good connections and no knowledge of modern problems.*

(quoted in P. Hennessy, *Whitehall*, Fontana. 1989)

- As Britain entered the Thatcher era in 1979 it was clear that the civil service would come under her microscope. One of Thatcher's advisers, **Sir John Hoskyns**, focused on recruitment as one of the civil service's main problems. He was particularly critical of the fact that all senior officials were internally promoted. They had, therefore, little or no experience of the worlds of business, commerce, industry or finance. They were, therefore, ill-equipped to bring a new business-like approach to administration which he, Mrs Thatcher and Sir Derek Rayner (head of the new Efficiency Unit) wished to see. The reforms which were to follow in the 1980s and 90s certainly need a new kind of civil servant to see them through.

## CURRENT RECRUITMENT AND PROMOTION SYSTEMS

There are two ways of looking at the characteristics of recruitment and promotion in the modern civil service. One is to consider the two hundred or so individuals who are recruited each year for 'fast stream' promotion to senior grades (i.e. the elite of the future). The other is to study the nature of the individuals who have reached the senior positions by the end of the century. We can then assess the extent to which the concerns described above have been addressed.

### *The Fast Stream*

Competition for the fast stream positions is intense. In 1998, for example, 9,037 applicants chased only 235 available posts. All of those appointed had excellent degrees and had passed through a rigorous selection procedure. Just under half were graduates of Oxford or Cambridge, a fact which can be interpreted in two ways. One is to suggest that the top levels of service continue to be recruited from a relatively narrow social background. The other – which is the 'official' explanation, is that since the positions require the most able people and Oxford and Cambridge attract most of Britain's best young brains, it is natural that a high proportion of their staff should be taken from there.

Some progress has been made to eliminate gender bias. In 1998 39% of fast stream appointments were women, still not parity, but a vast improvement on 1991 when the proportion of women was approximately 25%. As for members of ethnic minorities the record is starker, with only about 2% of entrants being from this group. (source: Cabinet Office)

The indications are, then, that the civil service still makes strenuous efforts to maintain high educational standards. However, there is still a bias towards 'traditional' educational backgrounds and towards white males. However, when we turn to examine the kind of people who are reaching the most senior levels we can find more significant changes.

### THE SENIOR CIVIL SERVICE

Here we should consider the five top grades known as the 'Senior Civil Service' (SCS). In April 1998 this comprised 3,720 individuals (including a small number of part time staff). These are the politically significant civil servants who are most directly involved in central government.

### *Women*

The first feature to note is the under-representation of women. 24% of SCS officials were women. If we consider the very highest rank – permanent secretary level – by the end of 1999 there were just two women in this position out of a total of 35.

### *Educational Background*

Here little change can be detected since Fulton reported in 1968. In the 1990s the vast majority of those appointed to the top three levels of the SCS had been educated at private schools (approximately 90%) and over 50% had graduated from either Oxford or Cambridge.

### *Career Background*

There has been a good degree of change here. This has largely been the result of the new policy, which came to fruition in the 1990s, of recruiting to the highest positions from *outside* the civil service. This is known as *lateral entry*. In practice a large number of senior posts are now openly advertised and there has been increasing recruitment from other fields such as banking, commerce and business. By 1999 lateral entry accounted for approximately one-third of senior appointments (many of which were to executive agencies rather than departmental posts). About 10% of those who reach the SCS do so by working their way up from lower grades. They make up a rare breed of individuals who usually have neither extensive outside experience or high levels of formal education. This leaves about 60% who were originally recruited as 'fast stream' entrants and who still largely conform to the traditional 'white-male-public school-Oxbridge' model of a senior civil servant

### Other Minorities

The civil service operates an equal  opportunities policy as strict as most other organisations. However, it remains true that in 1999 less than 2% of the SCS were from ethnic minorities and there were virtually no disabled representatives. Not surprisingly, figures do not exist indicating the extent to which the gay community is represented at the top levels of the service.

### Age

We would clearly not expect to find many very young men or women in senior positions. However, with the modern accent on a more dynamic, forward thinking service, with promotion based more on merit than on length of service, we might expect to find some movement towards greater youth in senior posts. Of the 90 individuals newly appointed to SCS posts in 1998, 22% were under 40 years of age. This shows little change since 1990. However, it should be noted that there has been a marked increase in the number of under-35s appointed here. The approximate average age of such new entrants to senior positions remained virtually constant during the 1990s at about 47. So there has been a little movement towards greater youth, but it is slow and will take time to work its way through the senior levels.

### Time Lags

We must be wary of drawing sweeping conclusions from the apparently slow rate of change in recruitment and promotion to the SCS. It is inevitable that changes taking place at the lower levels will take two decades before the effects are felt at the top. This does *not* apply to lateral entry, of course, where the effect has been immediate, but when we consider such factors as age, gender, background and minority status, reform must begin at lower levels and work its way upwards. The lack of women at higher levels is a useful illustration. The tiny number of female permanent secretaries reflects recruitment practices of the 1970s. We can assume that nearly 40% of women entrants to fast stream jobs in the late 1990s will be reflected at senior levels in twenty or so years time. In addition, the increased scope of lateral entry will also broaden the profile of the higher levels of the civil service.

### Political Appointments

The issue of how much political bias may play a part in promotion to senior levels is considered in some detail in Chapter 3. However, we should not leave this subject before making reference to it. The official position on this question is apparently clear and runs as follows:

> *There are a small number of very senior posts in which ministers will be closely interested because they are of considerable importance for the setting and delivery of their policies. Ministers have a legitimate interest in the kind of person who is appointed; but that interest must be accommodated within a system which produces appointments which can last into other Administrations and are free from personal or political bias.* (source: Office of the Civil Service Commissioners. *Guidance on Recruitment to senior civil service posts*)

It is therefore acceptable for political ministers to become involved in promotions, but their reasons for doing so are limited. As we shall see in the next chapter, the evidence suggests that there is relatively little or no bias in such appointments. However, there is also little doubt that ministers, *prime* ministers in particular, do prefer the kind of senior official who is best equipped to carry out their policies. In the Conservative years of 1979–97 this was likely to be an individual who accepted the disciplines of the free market and was willing to operate in a more business-like manner, who was dynamic and sympathetic to radical policies. For New Labour the accent remains similar but also encompasses the ability to adapt to constitutional changes, to more open and responsive government and to greater emphasis on the presentation as well as implementation of policy.

There is no doubt that change is afoot in these aspects of the civil service. The process will be aided by the fact that there does seem to be a new willingness within the service to accept criticisms and to be prepared to reform itself. Speaking in May 1999, Sir Richard Wilson, the Cabinet Secretary, demonstrated a candour and flexibility which has been all to rare in the past. He declared:

> *And we need to bring about a real culture change which values diversity. We have far too few women, people from black and ethnic minority backgrounds, and people with disabilities in the senior parts of the Civil Service. We must be part of, and not apart from, the society we serve. This is a top priority. We want a Civil Service which values the differences that people bring to it. We need to have the benefit of those differences. We must not only reflect the full diversity of society, but also be strengthened by that diversity.*

Source: Cabinet Office

# STUDY 🅟 GUIDE

## *Revision Hints*

It is vital that students of the subject have a clear idea of what the constitutional position of civil servants is. The anonymity, neutrality and permanence of the civil service must be clearly understood and its implications noted. Later there will be more discussion concerning the way in which these principles have come under threat, but at this stage it is more important to understand what they mean.

The nature of the relationship between ministers and civil servants is a crucial one. This involves knowing both what civil servants are expected to do and how this relates to the role of ministers. Finally the issues surrounding recruitment and promotion must be noted as these determine the make-up of the service and tell us much about how it is likely to behave.

## *Exam Hints*

Two particular kinds of question which relate to the material in this chapter are common. One asks students to describe the principles by which the civil service works and demands analysis of how these have changed in the modern political culture. The second issue deals with the relationships between ministers and civil servants. The concept of ministerial responsibility as it concerns this relationship must be understood. A later chapter will deal with the question of how much real power the civil service wields, but at this stage there are important questions about the differences between the political role of ministers and the administrative duties of civil servants.

## *Practice Questions*

1  What do you understand by the term 'individual ministerial responsibility'? How does it affect the role of civil servants?
2  Distinguish clearly between the role of ministers and that of civil servants. In what ways can this distinction become blurred?
3  To what extent is there genuinely open access to the civil service? Why is open access important for good government?

# 3

---

# CIVIL SERVICE POWER

## HOW COULD CIVIL SERVANTS INFLUENCE GOVERNMENT?

WE SAW IN Chapter 2 that British civil servants are theoretically neutral and that they are expected to give truly independent advice. Yet despite this, there have long been suspicions and accusations that senior civil servants have had a significant influence on official policies. We must ask here how this could be so and in the following two sections we will critically examine some of the claims.

The first factor to consider is that civil servants are permanent while governments and ministers are usually temporary (though the eighteen years of Conservative administration from 1979–1997 suggested otherwise). Senior officials have usually spent all their working life in the civil service, perhaps as long as forty or more years. Indeed in some cases, notably the Treasury, they may have stayed in the same department for all that time. This means they are experts on particular aspects of government. They understand the main issues, have an extensive grasp of relevant information and are familiar with the variety of individuals and groups who are concerned with politics. They are also expert administrators.

By contrast, ministers usually come to office with little experience of their new responsibility, often with little or no administrative experience and certainly scant knowledge of how the intricacies of government work. Furthermore the average length of service in an individual department is less than three years. Though writing many years ago, the Labour Cabinet Minister Richard Crossman can still perhaps demonstrate the best description of how it feels to be a new minister surrounded by experienced officials. He wrote thus in 1964 shortly after becoming Housing Minister, his first appointment:

---

*My Minister's room is like a padded cell, and in certain ways I am like a person who is suddenly certified a lunatic and put safely into this great, vast room, cut off from real life and surrounded by male and female trained nurses and attendants. When I am in a good mood they occasionally allow a normal human being to come and visit me; but they make sure that I behave right, and that the other person behaves right; and they know how to handle me.*

from Richard Crossman 1979, *The Crossman Diaries*. Magnum Books

---

Ever since Crossman's day, successive new ministers have struggled against their own inexperience in the face of the self-assured professionalism of their senior civil servants.

There are a variety of ways in which civil service influence over policy could manifest itself. Among them are the following features:

- imposing on new ministers established policies and practices within the department. This has been particularly marked in the Treasury where governments have fought to free economic policy making from that department's traditional reluctance to encourage public expenditure and legendary caution over financial policy;
- resistance to any radical policies. Civil Servants are not permitted to defy stated government policy and there is little evidence to suggest they do. Nevertheless, by stressing the negative aspects of new policies and constantly advocating a more cautious line, there is a possibility that ministers may well be forced to water down proposals. This may well have been the case when the Labour Government's plans for sweeping changes to the welfare system ran into difficulties in the late 1990s;
- manipulation of information may occur. Ministers rely on officials to supply them with the background facts upon which to base decisions. Skilful officials may be able to present statistics and research findings in such a way as to influence final conclusions;
- the TV series 'Yes Minister', referred to in Chapter 1, often showed civil servants hatching conspiracies with colleagues in other departments in order to get their own way. Though clearly an exaggeration for dramatic and comedy effect, many ministers, including Margaret Thatcher herself, privately admitted that the programmes may have contained some truth. It is often held that the Treasury, which has representatives in every department, works hard behind the scenes to ensure that policies do not prejudice their own economic and financial plans.

We can summarise the advantages which civil servants enjoy over government ministers in the following table:

| Table 4: *Advantages of Civil Servants* | |
|---|---|
| ADVANTAGES ENJOYED BY CIVIL SERVANTS | DISADVANTAGES SUFFERED BY MINISTERS |
| • Permanence | • Temporary appointment |
| • Professionalism | • Often no specialised knowledge |
| • Access to information | • Reliance on officials for information |
| • More time available | • Heavy workload |
| • Less political constraints | • Constrained by colleagues, etc. |

Above all, the fact that the civil servants endure while governments come and go is the greatest factor in their influence. Indeed, Professor Peter Hennessy, Britain's foremost commentator on the civil service refers to it as *permanent government*, which seems an apt expression.

Before leaving the subject a look at one of the scenes from 'Yes Minister' is worth viewing as an illustration, albeit a comic one, of civil service dominance. In this scene, Jim Hacker is the fictional minister and Sir Humphrey Appleby is his most senior official, the permanent secretary in the equally fictional Department of Administrative Affairs:

A SCENE FROM THE BBC TV SERIES 'YES MINISTER'

| | |
|---|---|
| Hacker: | What is it that I don't know? |
| Sir Humphrey: | What do you mean precisely? |
| Hacker: | I don't know... it's just that... there's something I don't know and I don't know because I can't find the right question to ask you because I don't know what to ask... What is it I don't know? |
| Sir Humphrey: | Minister, I don't know what you don't know. It could be almost anything. |
| Hacker: | But you are keeping things from me aren't you? |

He nodded... he explained that it is the Department's duty to protect the Minister from the great tide of irrelevant information that beats against the walls of the Department day and day.

(Adapted from The Complete *Yes Minister*. Jonathan Lynn and Anthony Jay. BBC Books 1989)

It is worth comparing this passage with the real words of Richard Crossman shown on page 34.

Whether or not the *potential* power of the civil service is still a significant factor in British political life must not be examined.

# THEORIES AND CRITICISMS OF CIVIL SERVICE POWER

Before describing the various theories which have flourished concerning the relationship between senior civil servants and different governments, we need to be clear about the term 'power'. If we adopt Professor Bernard Crick's definition of power as '*the ability to achieve premeditated ends*', then we will find that the civil service certainly does not wield power. However, if we replace the term power with the word 'influence' we may make progress. We know that civil servants give advice and in this sense they are bound to have some influence over decisions, even if they do not intend to. The real question the student of politics must ask, however, is whether there is any systematic attempt by civil servants to affect the way government makes its decisions. If there is, then civil servants do indeed exercise influence. Here are some theories on this subject:

1  **The Orthodox View**. This is that civil servants are indeed neutral in their dealings with government. That ministers are effectively in control and there is no premeditated attempt to subvert policy-making and implementation by the top civil service. Those who subscribe to this view – and that includes former prime ministers such as Harold Wilson – point out that governments with a number of different types of radical programmes have been able to carry them through. They would cite the extensive social, economic and industrial reforms of the 1940s, the revolutionary programme of the Thatcher

governments of the 1980s and a similarly radical set of policies adopted by new Labour after 1977. They suggest that the charge of excessive influence or interference by senior officials is designed to deflect attention away from the failures of ministers. Civil Servants only *appear* to be powerful when governments are weak, they say.

2 **The left Wing View**. This was popularised by the Labour Cabinet Minister Tony Benn and extensively described by a close colleague of his, Brian Sedgemore. Indeed Sedgemore's attack on the civil service almost amounted to a *conspiracy theory*. It was principally spawned from the experience of the Labour Governments of the 1960s and, to a lesser extent, 1950–51. The former entered office with proposals to modernise Britain. In particular there were plans to introduce more long-term and precise economic planning. This, they suggested, directly threatened the power of the greatest department of state, the Treasury. The creation of a new civil service department, the Department of Economic Affairs (DEA), staffed by specialist economists who were committed to the idea of centralised planning, was a direct challenge to Treasury power. When the idea of planning collapsed within two years, the sinister influence of the Treasury was immediately blamed by such left-wingers. A watered-down version of planning in the 1970s went the same way ten years later.

When the Fulton Committee recommended sweeping reforms of the Civil service in 1968, and when the attempt to implement them was thwarted, the case was proved, announced the anti-civil service lobby. There was, they argued, a permanent 'Establishment' in Britain which had controlled much of the state, including the law, the professions, government, the diplomatic service and the great financial institutions for many years. The 'Establishment' was made up of the representatives of a ruling class who maintained their influence by controlling these institutions and especially by determining who could enter them. Most importantly, they continued, the Establishment was utterly opposed to all forms of socialist policies. They used the civil service as the defence against their implementation. This was strong stuff, but it remained a popular view through the 1960s and 70s, only fading as the Conservative reforms of the 1980s took hold.

3 **The Right Wing View**. This idea has lingered in British politics throughout the post-war period, but was most forcefully promoted by Margaret Thatcher and her supporters. Far from being part of a Conservative Establishment, they declared, the civil service was dominated by characters who preferred to see the maintenance or extension of centralised state power. Many, indeed, might even have been closet socialists and left-wing intellectuals. They pointed to the creeping growth of the size of the state and its influence over society since the 1940s as clear proof of this. It did not need the election of Labour governments to ensure this spread of state power. The civil service had always been there to

sponsor it. Ammunition was provided in 1971–2 when the Conservative government under Edward Heath reversed its policies towards the state. Heath had arrived in office in 1970 with plans to dramatically scale down the role of the state, especially in the economic and industrial spheres. But within two years he has changed direction (this was known as the 'Heath U-Turn'). The hand of the civil service in these events was suspected.

The result of this view was, as we shall see in later chapters, the total reform of the civil service. Some argue it was a clear policy to change the personnel at the top of the civil service, to purge it of officials who would not accept the dramatic reductions in the state's functions which were to be effected.

4 **Other Views.** Close to the orthodox perspective is one to which Peter Hennessy has been sympathetic. This is the idea that the senior civil service tends to prefer policies which have **consensus** support, i.e. are widely supported in the country and do not alienate substantial parts of the population. This is a logical position to take as policies which do enjoy widespread support will be easier to implement. Some politicians, of course, may have mistaken the consensus position for active political opposition. It can also be observed that this is close to the constitutional role of civil servants. If they serve the state and the state will run better if there is consensus support for policies, then the position can be seen as a healthy one. The problem arises, however, if the ministers' view of consensus differs from that of his senior officials. The imposition of the disastrous and widely opposed poll tax in the late 1980s may have been a case in point.

5 **Departmentalism** is rather different. This is a tendency for individual departments to develop long term policies of their own. When a new minister of government comes to power, the theory runs, the department will seek to impose its own 'culture' upon them. This is often the theme of the *'Yes Minister'* programmes. The Treasury is most often suspected of such tactics. it is notoriously opposed to increased public expenditure or any radical spending plans. If the senior Treasury officials can persuade each new Chancellor of the Exchequer of the virtues of thrift, their influence automatically grows. In 1999, when Chancellor Gordon Brown was resisting calls for extensive increases in spending on health and education, some critics suggested he had 'gone native'. This phrase suggested that Brown had been influenced by the civil servants, adopting their norms of behaviour and so losing his enthusiasm for spending.

In a similar way there have been charges that the Department of Transport invariably favours the interests of private motorists over public transport and that Social Security civil servants prefer the traditional system of welfare delivery against the proposed reforms of 1998–9. In each case the civil service, so the argument continues, is like an oil tanker which will take a great deal of time and effort to change direction. Ministers therefore need to be both determined and patient if they are to carry their officials with them towards new initiatives. They will certainly need their co-operation.

Finally we come to a more serious charge. This sees the civil service as overtly political in its motivations. This is not to say that it is predominantly either left or right wing, as two of the theories described above have suggested. Here we see the civil service as open to undue influence by ministers, that it tends to lose its traditional neutrality and, like a chameleon, adapts too readily to the political environment and becomes the willing instrument of party rule. The reason why it might do this is to increase its influence by throwing its lot in with the powerful politicians of the day. This theory is known as **politicisation** and is dealt with in more depth in the next section.

# POLITICISATION OF THE CIVIL SERVICE

THEORIES

During the 1970s the emphasis in analysis of the civil service markedly changed. Models which suggested that the service wielded excessive power and that this was a negative element in British politics, were replaced by the so-called 'politicisation' theory. This suggested the opposite view that far from being an independent force, the civil service had allowed itself to become over-controlled by politicians. It was, therefore, losing its traditional independence and neutrality. This development, if true, was also seen as detrimental to Britain's political well-being.

David Richards, in his analysis of the civil service in 1979–97 (*The Civil Service under the Conservatives*. Sussex Academic Press. 1997) suggests three explanations of what happened to the service in the Thatcher years. These were:

1 **Overt Politicisation**

This theory – a minority opinion in Richards' view – was that Margaret Thatcher (1979–90) interfered with senior appointments and actively campaigned within the civil service to ensure that her radical brand of politics should prevail. Two important authorities can be quoted in support of the politicisation theory. One is Hugo Young, the other Nigel Lawson.

Young, a journalist, wrote possibly the best known account of Thatcherism. The title of this work – *One of Us* – illustrated a common view in the mid 1980s that, in order to be promoted as either a minister or civil servant, individuals had to pass Thatcher's test of being 'one of us'. What the phrase implied was that all senior officials should subscribe to her policies. Three key appointments to permanent secretary ships were made in 1983 which, Young suggests, indicated direct interference by Thatcher in order to promote her policies. it should be remembered that she had not then achieved the full dominance over government which she enjoyed after her election victory that year. The three were Peter Middleton (Treasury), Clive Whitmore (Defence) and Michael Quinton (Employment). In each case, Young argues, they were not the natural candidates for the posts but were publicly admired by Thatcher. He concludes that they were Thatcher's 'place-men'.

Lawson was Chancellor of the Exchequer between 1983 and 1989. In the course of his term in office he gradually became disillusioned with the economic policies being promoted by Thatcher, and also felt he was being undermined as a result of his opposition to her economic policies. He ultimately resigned as a result of disputes with a private adviser – Alan Walters – who was not a civil servant. Nevertheless his memoirs indicate that he suspected that his own civil servants had been subverted by Thatcherite ideas and that they preferred to serve those ideas rather than his own policies.

## 2 Management-Efficiency Ethos

This idea rejects the 'overt politicisation' thesis as a mistaken analysis of what went on in the 1980s. It suggests Margaret Thatcher did interfere with senior appointments and did try to change the nature of the civil service, but that this was in order to create a new style and management orientation within the

Sir Charles Powell, Margaret Thatcher's Private Secretary

service rather than simply to promote Conservative policies of the day. Richards detects this as a common view among ministers in the 1980s. It is also the view of Peter Hennessy. He stated firmly:

> *There was great turbulence among the personnel of the civil service and the methods used in fulfilling their routines. It is mistaken in my view to portray Mrs Thatcher as the politiciser of Whitehall and destroyer of the Gladstonian settlement [the Northcote-Trevelyan structure].*
>
> from Peter Hennessy. *Whitehall*. Fontana 1989

The term 'one of us', Hennessy suggests, really refers to the kind of individual whom Thatcher wished to promote in the civil service. These were dynamic, business-oriented', 'can-doers', rather than the conservative 'time-servers' whom she disparaged and suspected. Thatcher herself admitted that she wanted to push her own kind of people to senior positions, but denied that this amounted to politicisation. Referring to her desire to change the culture of the senior civil service, she wrote:

> *Those who came [to work in her private office] were some of the brightest young men and women in the civil service, ambitious and excited to be at the heart of decision-making in government. I wanted to see people of the same calibre, with lively minds and a commitment to good administration promoted to hold the senior posts in the department.*
>
> from M. Thatcher. *The Downing Street Years*. Harper-Collins 1993

## 3 Socialisation

Between the two previous theories the idea of socialisation suggests that civil servants are likely to gradually absorb the prevailing political climate and adapt to it. Those who are successfully 'socialised' in this way are more likely to be promoted to senior positions. We should remember that the Conservatives were in power for eighteen consecutive years, from 1979–97. It would be surprising, therefore, if most of the senior officials, much of whose career was spent under the same political party, should not share a similar outlook.

## POLITICISATION AND NEW LABOUR

If the more radical accounts of politicisation under the Conservatives were true, the new Labour administration which took over in May 1997 would have encountered severe problems with the civil service. It would, the theory suggests, have inherited a civil service steeped in Thatcherite, right wing policies and resistant to the more extreme policies of the incoming party. In the event no such difficulty occurred. On the contrary, the transition from Conservatism to New Labour appeared to happen so smoothly that central administration seemed hardly affected. Of course the new government was aided by the fact that many senior civil servants chose the moment to retire or to seek alternative employment. This meant that a large amount of new blood could be introduced by the new ministers. At the same time, the Cabinet Secretary, Sir Robin Butler, who was also due for retirement, stayed on to help with the take-over. He had, indeed, ensured that full consultation by senior officials had taken place with prospective Labour ministers long before the election confirmed what everybody suspected – that the Conservatives would lose office in 1997.

This is not to say that the changeover occurred without any controversy. New Labour proved determined – some would say obsessed – with achieving a consensus on their policies and with ensuring that information reaching the media and the public should be carefully controlled. The new issue was whether civil servants would be asked to *promote* (as opposed to merely advise and implement) government policies, a role which has traditionally been forbidden? The activities of the prime minister's press secretary (a civil service post), Alastair Campbell, certainly appeared to be pushing hard against the principle of neutrality. This recalled the Thatcher-Bernard Ingham partnership in the 1980s, described in the final section of this chapter. Indeed by 1999 the Blair and Campbell families were even taking their summer holiday together! The traditional distance which normally exists between ministers and civil servants was apparently narrowing. A number of existing press secretaries working for other departments also resigned in 1997–8 for fear of losing their independence.

However, it is not politicisation which has brought anxiety to the civil service under New Labour. Rather, it is the growth in the use of special advisers who have been brought in to advise and promote the government and the Labour party itself which has caused concern. These special advisers, who are *not* civil servants, numbered over fifty by the end of the century. There are new fears of tension growing between the overtly *political* advisers and the traditionally *neutral* senior civil service. In order to try to prevent this kind of politicisation the *relationships* between civil servants and special advisers or lobbyists are now included in the *Codes of Conduct* governing the behaviour of civil servants. The recommendations of the **Nolan Report** into the conduct of public life, which first appeared in 1995, forbade the following practices:

- The leaking of sensitive material to advisers or lobbyists
- Granting privileged access to ministers to outsiders
- Granting special privileges to private advisers

Nevertheless it remains true that relationships between special advisers and civil servants is a difficult one. To some extent the new style of 'Joined-Up government', announced by the government in 1998 (described in Chapter 4), sanctions closer links between the two. Policy making will, the new principles suggest, involve civil servants and such outsiders working *together*, not against each other. This may lead to a further blurring between the neutral civil service and the growing army of political advisers.

## THE DANGERS OF POLITICISATION

If politicisation has or is occurring we must ask what problems would arise? These can be summarised as follows:

- The civil service is required to serve the national interest. If it fails to do so because it has been politically subverted to the interests of solely the ruling party, it will be unable to carry out this duty.
- There may be a blurring of the distinction between the interests of the *government* and those of the *ruling party*. These are not the same thing, though it is true that the government is made up of leading members of the ruling party. The difference is that the government is expected to serve the country, whereas the ruling party serves itself. If civil servants begin to further the interests of the *party*, which they may do if they have been politicised, then democracy is being damaged. Civil servants are neither elected nor publicly accountable so they should stay clear of the political arena.
- If civil servants are promoted to senior levels on the basis of their political beliefs, there is a danger that the more able individuals will be passed over in favour those who are sympathetic to the ruling party. This does not serve the interests of good, impartial administration.

### *Conclusions on Politicisation*

As the 1997 election approached and it became clear that Labour was going to win, the question was asked again and again whether the new government would be able to work with a civil service which had known only Conservative rule for eighteen years. Every senior civil servant had been promoted to their position by Conservative ministers. Some had spent over half their career under the Conservatives. The question which Peter Hennessy asked at the time was whether the senior civil service had become 'Bluehall' instead of Whitehall. Supporting this fear, former prime minister James Callaghan suggested in 1992 that the civil service was so imbued with New Right, Thatcherite Conservatism that any new Labour government would experience great difficulties with it.

In the event, the transition was relatively smooth. There were few complaints of obstruction from the new labour ministers. Indeed it seemed that the civil service had captured the new spirit of reform with some enthusiasm. The main cloud on the horizon has been civil service resistance to a radical Freedom of Information Act, but this could have been expected under any administration. The case for politicisation appears, as David Richards has argued in his study of the civil service under the Conservatives, to be largely unproven.

Richards does, however, conclude that civil servants themselves felt that they were expected to support ministers and the government rather more slavishly than in the past. Where once they might have been expected to be critical or even sceptical of ministers' plans, in the national interests, they were now pressured to accept policy uncritically. The emphasis has therefore changed from development of sound policies to enthusiastic implementation of policy. The admired tradition in the civil service of great minds developing and refining policy was thus eroded. The new senior civil servants were to be activists rather than thinkers.

Wherever the truth lies, in the event, when Labour took power in 1997 the transition seemed to be remarkably smooth. The Blair administration wanted the same kind of dynamic individuals in the civil service which Conservative governments had favoured. Cynics will also suggest that the *substance* of New Labour policies was also little changed from those of the outgoing Major government. Adjustments for senior officials were, therefore, minimalised.

## WHOM DO CIVIL SERVANTS SERVE?

At first sight this seems to be a redundant question. They are servants of the Crown and the Crown represents the state. So they serve the state. But the question then arises – who shall judge what is in the best interests of the state? This question was brought into focus by the Ponting case which is described in the next section. Ponting brought a response from the then Cabinet Secretary, Sir Robert Armstrong, who issued the so-called 'Armstrong Memorandum' in 1985. This states the following:

> *Civil Servants are servants of the Crown... For all practical purposes the Crown in this context means and is represented by the Government of the day. The Civil Service as such has no constitutional personality of responsibility separate from the duly elected Government of the day.*

In other words it is not for civil servants to decide what is or is not in the interests of the state, they must always ask for guidance from their minister.

Unfortunately, the Armstrong memorandum and the civil service code, (which has been updated since), does not help a civil servant being asked to act in a manner which serves the ruling party rather than the state, or is possibly being asked to mislead others, or to become involved in the internal politics of the government. He may take his case to the highest authority, the Cabinet Secretary possibly, but risks being told simply to go away and do his minister's bidding. Only when he is being asked to act illegally does a civil servant have the absolute right to refuse to act.

We can now see that morality, national interest and political neutrality are all threatened by the principles of the Armstrong memorandum. To some extent this is the result of a system which insists on the anonymity of civil servants and does not allow them to be held accountable for what they do or for the advice they give. If they were capable of being called to account personally by parliament, for example, it might be possible for them to make a case for acting against the expressed wishes of a minister. As things stand they cannot. They must serve the minister faithfully and must accept his version of government policy and the national interest.

CIVIL SERVICE CASE STUDIES

This selection is chosen to illustrate some of the questions raised earlier in this chapter:

### Clive Ponting

Ponting was a middle ranking civil servant in the Defence Ministry. In 1985 he became convinced that his minister – Michael Heseltine – had misled parliament over information concerning Britain's conduct in part of the Falklands War of 1992. He therefore leaked the 'truth' – as he saw it – to the Guardian newspaper. Ponting believed he was acting in the 'public interest' and was therefore justified in his actions. He was prosecuted under the Official Secrets Act for publishing secret information against the wishes of the minister. Ponting repeated his defence – that he had a higher duty than to his minister; his duty was to the national interest. The judge did not accept this as a defence and attempted to instruct the jury that Ponting had no valid defence. As it happened the jury decided to acquit Ponting (a decision about which lawyers still disagree as to whether it was justified or not) but the effect of the case was to clarify the position for officials.

Despite his acquittal, Ponting was dismissed and the Cabinet Secretary, Sir Robert Armstrong, decided to re-state the principle that civil servants have no right to interpret the national interest in a different way to that of their minister. This was the 'Armstrong Memorandum' which guides the conduct of all officials. The effect of Ponting's case was to confirm what was already known – that civil servants must serve ministers uncritically and must not make their own decisions in sensitive issues.

### Colette Bowe

Shortly after the Ponting case a dispute broke out in the Cabinet between Michael Heseltine in Defence and Leon Brittan, who was Trade Minister. This was over the proposed purchase of helicopters for the armed forces. The incident became known as the 'Westland Affair'. Bowe was Brittans' Head of Information in his department. On his orders she 'leaked' a letter from the Solicitor General which would help with Brittan's case against Heseltine. The leak was revealed in early 1986 as a result of which Brittan was forced to resign (one of the last examples of a minister taking full responsibility for his actions by resigning), as was Heseltine. Ironically Bowe survived the incident on the grounds that she was following her boss's orders.

The Bowe case illustrates what can happen if civil servants are dragged into internal political disputes in government. Their position, especially their neutrality, is compromised and the process of government falls into disrepute.

## Bernard Ingham

Inghan, a press officer under the previous Labour government, was appointed as prime minister Margaret Thatcher's press secretary in 1979, a position he held until her removal from power in 1990. As the years went by it became increasingly apparent that Ingham was serving Mrs Thatcher personally rather than the government as a whole. Indeed, there were occasions when Ingham's version of policy differed from that of other ministers in the government. In other words he appeared to be operating for Thatcher *against* her own colleagues. His press briefings became legendary. A number of privileged journalists were regularly invited to hear Margaret Thatcher's views on the political scene conveyed to them by Ingham. It became increasingly difficult to distinguish between Ingham's views and those of the prime minister.

The behaviour of Bernard Ingham was principally responsible for charges that the civil service under Thatcher had become clearly politicised. Ingham became less and less shy in expressing his admiration for prevailing policies. Thus, not only was his neutrality compromised, but also the principle of anonymity.

## Alastair Campbell

ALASTAIR CAMPBELL, TONY BLAIR'S PRESS SECRETARY

Campbell, like Ingham, was appointed prime minister's press secretary when Tony Blair came to power in 1997. He exemplifies New Labour's determination to control information coming out of government. Campbell has extended responsibility for the whole information machinery of government and is allowed access to all government papers in all departments. Campbell's position has gone one step beyond that of Ingham. Not only is he the prime minister's spokesman, he is also in overall charge of government information. He is, therefore, in a strong position to exert the prime minister's control over the whole government.

Although the Labour government has over 70 non-civil servants as overtly political advisers and information officers, Alastair Campbell, who is a civil servant and therefore theoretically bound by its disciplines, has rekindled fears that the civil service is being expected to serve the interests of the ruling party and not just the government.

### *Armd to Iraq and the Scott Report*

It became apparent during 1995 that there had been serious irregularities in arms sales to the Saddam Hussein régime in Iraq. In particular it was revealed that the government was sanctioning such sales even though official government policy was to ban them. The political crisis which the revelations created led to an inquiry under Lord Justice Richard Scott. The **Scott report** produced a number of damning criticisms of ministers but also uncovered civil service practices which were viewed as unacceptable. It seemed that officials had co-operated with ministers in misleading parliament and the public and were effectively carrying out a policy – to supply arms to Iraq – which was technically illegal. This echoed the crisis of conscience which Clive Ponting had experienced ten years before. Further problems over Foreign Office policy towards a civil war in Sierra Leone in 1997–8, suggest that few lessons have been learned since the Ponting and Scott cases. It remains unclear how civil servants should behave if they are required faithfully to serve ministers who are acting illegally, or at least in contradiction to national interest or are actively misleading parliament.

STUDY GUIDE

Students should construct first a set of notes which describe precisely the potential ways in which the civil service *might* exercise power and influence. This should be reinforced by a clear understanding of all the theories which abound about civil service power. In each case as many illustrations should be added, either from this book or from other sources. The case studies described are of social importance here. It is important to note that there are as many arguments suggesting that the civil service has limited influence as there are arguing that it is powerful.

The issue of politicisation is both important and topical. Here evidence of the process should be noted, together with arguments suggesting it may be over-exaggerated. Again illustration should be noted. Alongside the debate about politicisation lies the issue of whom civil servants serve. The various theories should be noted and the case studies used to underpin the discussion.

Discussion of how much power and influence the civil service really wields is one of the commonest questions in modern politics examinations. Students should be prepared to tackle it. The use of examples and knowledge of the various important authorities on the subject such as Crossman or Hennessy is vital in such questions. Almost as popular are questions on politicisation. These ask the extent to which it exists and sometimes may ask why it is important. Here again, case studies and illustrations must accompany a strong answer. Answers about both power and politicisation should balance different sides of the Arguments, but should also come to a firm conclusion.

1  How much political power does the civil service wield?
2  Assess the argument suggesting that the British civil service has become so politicised since 1979 that it can no longer be described as neutral.
3  Whom do civil servants serve? Whom *should* they serve?

# 4

# CIVIL SERVICE REFORM SINCE 1968

## THE FULTON COMMITTEE — THE FAILED REFORMS

### *What Fulton found*

THE LABOUR GOVERNMENT which came to power under Harold Wilson in 1964 was committed to a programme of modernisation for Britain. They hoped to see progress on economic planning, industrial technology, improved industrial relations and an overhaul of the whole education system. Wilson suspected that the civil service, which would have to implement these changes, was not equipped for the task. He therefore set up a committee under Lord Fulton to investigate and make recommendations. The committee began work in 1966 and reported in 1968.

Fulton produced a largely damning indictment of the civil service. Among its wide variety of comments were the following principle criticisms:

- civil servants were recruited from narrow social, educational and career backgrounds. They did not, therefore, have a wide enough perspective on modern problems;
- most senior civil servants were what they called 'generalists'. That is to say they had little or no specialist knowledge in such areas as economics, planning, science, engineering, education and the like. They were essentially 'amateurs' in many areas. By the same token, too few specialists or experts were promoted to senior posts;
- civil servants were expected to pick up administrative skills through long service. There was little or no opportunity for specialist training in management and administration;
- the organisation of the civil service as a whole was controlled by the Treasury. As the Treasury was seen as an essentially conservative body, there was an in-built resistance to change;

- promotion tended to be based more on long service than on merit;
- the civil service failed to assess and modify its own performance. It did not make judgements about its own efficiency and effectiveness, as businesses have to do.

### *What Fulton suggested*

1 There should be more opportunities for specialists to reach senior positions. Indeed, Fulton recommended that each job should be evaluated and the most appropriately qualified person appointed to do that job. If this required specialist knowledge then the post holder would have to have it.

2 Recruitment should be opened up to a wider variety of applicants. In particular many senior posts should be opened up to applicants from fields *outside* the civil service. This was known as lateral entry. This would inject new blood into the service and people with more knowledge and experience of the outside world. In addition they suggested that civil servants should spend short periods on 'secondment' to other jobs, for example in private banking or business, to gain experience. Similarly there should be opportunities for outsiders to be seconded *into* the civil service.

3 General control of the civil service should be removed from the Treasury and given to a new Civil Service Department under the control of the prime minister.

4 A Civil Service College should be set up to train civil servants in administrative skills.

5 Each department of government should have a 'Planning Unit' headed by an appropriate specialist. These units were to deal with long term policy planning.

6 Each department should set up an organisation to monitor their own efficiency.

This set of recommendations was extremely radical and shocked the civil service to such a degree that it set up a campaign to thwart its intentions. Indeed the civil service's reaction to Fulton was, in some ways, more significant than the committee's criticisms themselves. Margaret Thatcher, the next prime minister to take on the civil service, did not fall into the same trap as Wilson's government. The mistake after Fulton was to expect the civil service to *reform itself*. Thatcher learned from this and brought in outsiders to do the job.

### *What happened after Fulton*

Essentially the changes made after Fulton were largely cosmetic. The principal developments and their failings can be seen through the following table:

| Table 5: *Changes resulting from the Fulton report* | |
|---|---|
| FULTON PROPOSAL | ACTION TAKEN |
| To expose recruitment and promotion to all in a single open service and allow lateral entry at senior levels | The service did become unified but open recruitment and promotion did not become a reality. Senior positions remained limited to a narrow group of career civil servants. Few lateral entries or secondments were allowed |
| Creation of a Civil Service Department | Set up, but dominated by former Treasury officials so it became a very conservative body, opposed to radical reform. It was abolished in 1981 |
| The Civil Service College | Set up, but largely ran short, low-level course to junior ranking civil servants. |
| Promotion of more specialists to senior posts | In theory top posts were opened to specialists, but in practice very few were actually promoted. |
| Monitoring for efficiency to be introduced | Only small low level units set up |

In short, most or all of Fulton's recommendations were either ignored or watered down to such an extent as to be ineffective. Nevertheless Fulton did prepare the ground for future change. It did this in two main ways. Firstly it opened up informed debate about the problems of the civil service in the modern world. Secondly, the experience of its failures instructed future reformers how *not* to go about reform. The post-Fulton mistakes were not repeated.

THE RAYNER REFORMS

When Margaret Thatcher came to power in 1979 her reforming attention turned almost immediately to the institution which had successfully resisted ten years before. Thatcher attacked the entrenched practices and attitudes in the civil service with such enthusiasm for a number of reasons:

- she wished to reduce public expenditure as quickly as possible. This was partly to finance tax cuts and partly to make more public money available for productive investment. As a sign of her intentions she announced, as one of her first acts in government, an immediate freeze on fresh recruitment to the service to fill vacancies;
- Thatcher was committed ideologically to reducing the size and scope of government. She believed that 'too much government' was intrinsically a bad thing and held back progress;

- she took an almost instant dislike to dominant attitudes among top civil servants. She saw them as over-conservative, resistant to change and inefficient. They were, she observed, very keen to be involved in developing policy, but hopelessly reluctant to take responsibility for implementing and managing services effectively.

As an illustration of her feelings about the civil senior service we can review her own description of a dinner she arranged for most of the permanent secretaries in May 1980:

---

*This was one of the most dismal occasions of my entire time in government. I enjoy frank and open discussion, even a clash of temperaments and ideas, but such a menu of complaints and negative attitudes as was served up that evening was enough to dull any appetite I may have had for this kind of occasion in the future. The dinner took place a few days before I announced civil service cuts in the Commons, and that was presumably the basis of complaints that ministers had damaged civil service morale.*

(source: Margaret Thatcher. *The Downing Street Years*. Harper Collins 1993)

---

In order to deal with civil service reform Thatcher set up an *Efficiency Unit*, placing at its head the managing director of her favourite company, Marks and Spencer. This was Sir Derek Rayner. Backed by a young team of enthusiastic reformers led by Clive Priestly, the unit undertook a grand tour of the civil service to establish how it could be streamlined and made more efficient.

After three years of intensive scrutiny, the Rayner exercise resulted in three main developments:

1  Overmanning had been identified in many areas, so the process of reducing the sheer size of the civil service could begin. Between 1979–82, when Rayner left the Efficiency Unit to return to Marks and Spencer, the number of civil servants fell from 735,000 to 669,000. When Mrs Thatcher left office in 1990 the number had fallen further to 567,000.

2  Under the guidance of Michael Heseltine, who was Secretary of State for Environment, a system known as 'MINIS' was introduced in many departments. MINIS stands for 'Management Information System for Ministers', a device to enable each minister to know exactly what were the responsibilities of each of his officials, and which established a method of assessing costs and the quality of performance. It was, in other words, a close copy of the kind of management control which existed in most private business organisations.

3  The Financial Management Initiative (FMI) was developed. The MINIS system had provided ministers with information and FMI was a way in which they could act upon that information to improve the performance of their department. Departments, sections and individual civil servants were given

specific tasks, targets and priorities. These included assessments of acceptable costs and ways of measuring performance against those costs. Incentives were introduced to encourage officials to meet the targets set by the FMI. These incentives included a combination of improved promotion prospects and increased salary. As with MINIS, the FMI was seen as the way successful businesses operate.

Most commentators have seen the Rayner reforms of 1979–82 as relatively mild. They did reduce civil service numbers markedly, did reduce expenditure on the central bureaucracy and did begin the process of changing civil service attitudes, but they did not alter the basic *structure* of the service. It was seen that they did not tackle a fundamental issue. This was the distinction between the part of the civil service which was concerned with *policy* and that which was concerned with management. We have seen that Thatcher and Rayner believed that civil servants tended to concern themselves with policy work at the expense of sound management. But the question was how to separate the two functions. This was left to Rayner's successor, Robin Ibbs.

IBBS AND THE 'NEXT STEPS'

*The Nature and Extent of Reform*
The Efficiency Unit was taken over from Rayner by Sir Robin Ibbs, also a businessman, in 1982. Few members of the general public have heard of Ibbs yet he instituted possibly the most radical reform of the machinery of central government in the whole of the twentieth century.

Ibbs recognised that the management functions of the civil service could be significantly improved if there were to be *institutional* changes in the way it was organised. He therefore proposed the splitting of the policy side of the bureaucracy from its management side. The latter was to be carried out by a new kind of body to be known as an **executive agency**. These agencies, responsible for the management and delivery of services, but not involved in the process of making government policy, were to be organised very much like private businesses. The report which made these recommendations as a follow-up to FMI was published in 1988, entitled **The Next steps.** It was quickly accepted by the Thatcher government. Sir Peter Kemp, a leading civil servant and supporter of the reforms, was selected to push through the 'Next Steps' programme.

Each executive agency was headed by a chief executive whose salary, terms and conditions were negotiated separately from other senior civil servants. This was also true of the agency's senior management. Recruitment was mostly from the existing civil service, but managers were free to appoint appropriate staff from elsewhere. Agencies were given financial targets to meet and were expected to introduce monitoring systems to govern their own efficiency. Incentives were introduced to encourage agency staff to meet their objectives. Although ministers and their most senior civil servants would oversee the work of the agencies, they would be essentially independent of political control. To complete the picture, the Next Steps Agencies, as they were often described, were free to contract out some of their work to private firms if they believed this would cut costs and/or improve efficiency.

Since 1988 the agency system has proved popular with ministers of both Conservative and Labour governments. The Civil Service itself, once so opposed to reform, has also come into line.

By April 1999, 135 of these agencies had come into existence, employing 324,045 staff. Four other sections of the civil service were not technically agencies, but had come to be run on the same lines. This brought the total number of employees to 383,400. In other words most civil servants were now employed by agencies rather than directly by government departments. The table below shows some of the biggest of the Next Steps agencies:

| Table 6: *The Largest 'Next Steps' Agencies as at April 1999* | |
| --- | --- |
| AGENCY | NUMBER OF EMPLOYEES |
| Social Security Benefits Agency | 66,295 |
| Inland revenue | 57,080 |
| Prison Service | 39,365 |
| Employment Service | 28,610 |
| Customs and Excise | 23,400 |
| Army Training and Recruiting | 12,020 |

Source: Cabinet Office

In addition to these the Labour Government announced that, during 1999 it intended to transfer a further 13 services to agency status, employing a further 21,565 peopie. So the process continues. When Robin Ibbs first instituted the changes, he passed the opinion that it might ultimately be possible to reduce the total size of the old civil service to a staggeringly low 20,000 officials dealing directly with policy. All the rest, he suggested, might be employed by agencies.

### *The Agencies Assessed*

The first thing to say about this reform is that it has, unlike its predecessors, been accepted by the civil service. It has also enjoyed cross-party support. These two facts alone indicate some level of success. There have also been further reductions in the number of people employed by government, partly as a result of savings made by the agencies. They are estimated to have met about three quarters of their targets and have successfully managed a number of useful privatisations. Several services, such as the Inland Revenue and the Social Security Benefits Agency have been able to streamline their service to the public.

Yet there have also been high profile failures. The Child Support Agency, which seeks to recover child maintenance costs from absent parents, proved to be so inadequate and unpopular in its operation that it had to be effectively dissolved and re-formed in 1998. The Prison Service experienced major failures and embarrassments in the mid-1990s and the Passport Agency simply failed to cope with demand during 1999, much to the discomfort of the Home Office.

These well-publicised problems brought into focus one of the key political issues in relation to the agency system. The traditional principle that government ministers should be responsible for the actions of the civil servants in their departments was suddenly undermined. Beginning with Home Secretary Michael Howard's assertion that he would not be held accountable for failures in the Prison Service in 1994, it became clear that the position of parliament was likely to be significantly weakened. If ministers were to claim that they would not be responsible for the performance of those agencies which came under their oversight, how could MPs impose sanctions for errors and weak performance? They were certainly not in a position to dismiss or censure the staff responsible for the mistakes.

On the another hand, the traditional anonymity of the civil service was destroyed when officials were transferred to agencies. Furthermore the security of tenure – which gave civil servants the virtual certainty of knowing their jobs were safe no matter what – no longer existed in the agencies. In some senses this can be seen as a positive step. The threat of dismissal or of a ruined career might improve performance. Conversely, however, the pressure of greater openness and loss of job security might result in lack of innovation and independence among senior executives.

It is too early to make a clear assessment of the agencies either in terms of financial efficiency or of democratic control. However, the early indications are that improved effectiveness may be being achieved at the expense of political responsibility.

## THE CITIZEN'S CHARTER AND MARKET TESTING

Prime minister John Major, who took over from Thatcher in 1990, was determined to maintain the pace of reform set by his predecessor. Not only did he continue to allow the creation of more executive agencies, he was determined to introduce a new *culture* into the civil service. He was concerned that officials tended to lack two vital qualities. One was a drive to be more efficient, the other was awareness that they were there to serve the public and thus should concentrate on quality of service. Both these disciplines flourished in private industry, why should they not do so in government?

The **Citizens' Charter** idea was launched in 1991. Here a wide variety of public services, run by such bodies as local authorities, the National Health Service, public corporations, executive agencies and government departments, were now required to aim for maximum standards of service. Among the major services to be subjected to Charter targets were public transport, the Inland Revenue (taxation) and The Benefits Agency. In many cases performance targets were set and monitoring introduced to see whether these targets were being met. In some cases it was even possible for members of the public to seek financial compensation if a service was unsatisfactory. Above all, however, the Citizens' Charter was designed to ensure that public employees and managers should adopt a new attitude to their work. They should be less inward looking and instead consider the *effects* of their work on citizens. In other words the Next Steps agencies had created *institutional* change, and the Citizens' Charter was to encourage *attitudinal* change.

A follow-up to the Charter was the principle of **Market Testing**. Here departments and agencies were required to analyse the performance of a large number of their services. They were to compare their economic efficiency with that of private companies providing a similar service. The result of such an exercise was *either* to accept that the private sector was more efficient and so transfer responsibility for the service to them *or* to bring the department's own efficiency level up to that of the private sector. Public services are not normally subject to market forces, but market testing was designed to imitate the effects of the free market, with similar results.

Extravagant claims were immediately made for the success of market testing. Either through internal savings or by privatisation of services, hundreds of millions of pounds were claimed to have been saved. However true or exaggerated these claims may be, the way in which the civil service thinks of itself has certainly been radically and permanently changed.

JOINED UP GOVERNMENT — THE NEW LABOUR INITIATIVES

### *The New Approach to Policy Making*

The Labour Government which came to power in 1997 quickly made it clear that they accepted the ongoing reforms which had been instituted under Margaret Thatcher and John Major since 1979. Though less emphasis was placed on market testing and the Citizens' Charter received less emphasis, the general thrust of change was maintained. As we have seen above, Labour also continued to create new executive agencies. But a new direction was also needed.

Tony Blair turned his attention back to the question of policy making. The spotlight now turned to the three thousand or so senior civil servants who were most closely involved in the policy development process. What Blair and his advisers saw was a service dedicated to developing initiatives designed to further the objectives of *individual* government departments and their ministers. In other words, senior civil servants were not taking a general *overview* of key problems, but were instead merely looking at the work of their own department.

A good example concerns the phenomenon of **Social Exclusion**. This relates to the problems associated with those individuals and families who have found themselves excluded from mainstream society for a number of reasons. They key factor is that the problems of such people are *plural*. There is not one single cause of their deprivation, but a whole series of causes. These embrace such issues as poor education, housing, health care, family support, unemployment or low wages and a variety of other factors. It follows that the solutions to these problems are also plural.

Examples of other areas which are being subjected to this kind of *holistic* – i.e. integrated rather than fragmented – approach to policy making have included:

- competitiveness in Industry and Commerce – to try to ensure consumers are being fairly treated;
- transport – an attempt to integrate policies on roads, road safety, alternatives to the motor car, environment problems, public transport, etc;
- government regulation – a common approach to the ways in which government institutions regulate industry and commerce;
- air quality control;
- women's rights;
- the 'Sure Start' programme designed to help those children under four years old who are suffering various kinds of deprivation.

### The Comprehensive Spending Review

Underpinning the approach has been the **Comprehensive Spending Review**. This was introduced in 1998. It is a new and more thorough way of examining public spending. It has been designed to achieve two objectives:

1 It requires all section and departments to evaluate the way in which they spend money. The review embraces not only efficiency, but also examines where further privatisation or sales of government assets might be beneficial and may include necessary organisational changes.

2 Possibly more importantly, spending will not be simply reviewed on a department-by-department basis, but will be considered in terms of each complete policy area. Thus, the kind of policy areas listed above will be subjected to expenditure planning and individual departments will have to fit in with those plans.

### *The Centre for Management and Policy Studies*

This is an attempt to revive some of the more ambitious plans for the Civil Service College which had been set up after the Fulton Report in 1968. It is an attempt to bring together all the best management techniques which can be identified in both the private and the public sectors. Civil Servants are invited to be trained in these techniques and to take them back to their departments.

In some ways it represents the introduction, albeit on a less ambitious scale, of the kind of business qualifications which are valued in the private sector. It implies that the same kind of organisational and management techniques which business requires can be applied to public services. It is also intended that the more flexible and innovative approaches to policy making to be introduced will enhance movement to 'joined-up' government.

### *An assessment of New Labour's Reforms*

The new approach will require a change in the culture of the civil service possibly as great as that required by the Ibbs reforms. This is how the White Paper, *Modernising Government*, put it in March 1999:

---

*This Government expects more of policy makers. More new ideas, more willingness to question inherited ways of doing things, better use of evidence and research in policy making and better focus on policies that will deliver long term goals. Our challenge … is to get different parts of government to work together, where that is necessary, to deliver the Government's overall strategic objectives.*

Source: White Paper, *Modernising Government*, Cm. 4310 March 1999

---

In other words, it represents an attempt to change the way in which the senior civil service thinks about policy. This change echoed the criticisms Peter Hennessy made ten years earlier and which were described in Chapter 3. An illustration of the new vision of the civil service can be demonstrated by the quote from a job advertisement shown opposite.

It may be that these high minded and well-intentioned reforms go the way of Fulton thirty years before. They challenge entrenched attitudes and practices in the civil service. Above all they promise to attack the security of officials who understood that they were to serve their own department's interests and could leave it to others to worry about overall government strategy. There are some, including members of the government itself, who believe that further *institutional* change may also be necessary.

It may also be that the ambition to change the nature of civil service policy–making in so comprehensive a way, and in such a short space of time, is over-optimistic. At the same time as new policy–thinking is being encouraged, the systems of recruitment and promotion are also becoming more flexible. A more dynamic service may indeed be needed but this threatens to be at the expense of

*Help Create the Civil Service of the 21st Century*

# Senior Adviser

Up to £73, 470 (more may be available for an exceptional candidate)

*'The Civil Service must be part of, not apart from, the society it serves'.*

Are you the person to help make this happen? Can you spearhead efforts to improve the number and profile of people from ethnic minority backgrounds in the Civil Service?

The Government wants the Civil Service to represent all of the cultures and ethnic minority backgrounds which make up our society. Reporting to the Head of the Civil Service and the Minister for the Cabinet Office this senior appointment will spearhead efforts to improve the number and profile of ethnic minorities in the Service.

This is a key, top level post. It needs someone who has:

- a strong track record as a campaigner and enabler of change
- a real understanding of large organisations and their dynamics
- the drive to define a strategy and underpin it with practical action
- the ability to communicate persuasively in a variety of contexts.

This is a 3 year fixed term appointment with the possibility of extension or permanency. It is available on either a full or part-time basis (dependent on the most suitable applicant) and a secondment would be considered. Relocation expenses may be available.

Source: A T Kearney, *The Guardian* 8/9/99

security. It could be argued that public servants who lack a sense of security may make poor decisions.

On the other hand the Labour reforms announced since 1997 can also be seen merely as a continuation of the processes which had gone before. In other words, they may not be as radical as they first appear.

## A SUMMARY OF REFORMS SINCE 1968

The table below summarises the reforms described above.

| Table 7: *Civil Service reforms since 1968* | | |
|---|---|---|
| REFORM | PERIOD | NATURE OF REFORMS |
| Fulton | 1968–70 | Mild reorganisation<br>Civil Service College<br>Civil Service Department<br>Slightly more flexible recruitment and promotion system. |
| Rayner | 1979–82 | Reduction in size<br>Drive for greater efficiency<br>MINIS introduced<br>Financial Management Initiative (FMI) initiated. |

| REFORM | PERIOD | NATURE OF REFORMS |
|---|---|---|
| Ibbs | 1988–present | Transfer of services to more independent executive agencies. |
| Citizens' Charter | 1991–present | Target standards of service established and performance monitored. |
| Market Testing | 1992–present | Comparing efficiency and effectiveness with private sector. Some privatisation of services. |
| Joined-Up government | 1998–present | More long-term, cross-cutting, integrated policies across departmental lines |

We are now in a position to consider the extent to which there are consistent themes during the whole period since 1968. In so far as they do exist they appear to include the following trends:

- greater flexibility and openness in recruitment and promotion systems;
- introduction of management and administration techniques which are similar to those used in private sector organisations;
- decentralisation of service provision away from big Whitehall departments to a range of other bodies with varying degrees of independence from government;
- clear separation between the small policy-making part of the civil service and the larger sections which are concerned with delivering services;
- greater emphasis on giving service to the public in a sensitive and effective manner;
- increased opportunities to private services formerly monopolised by the public (i.e. government) sector.

We must also summarise the *effects* of these reforms on the way in which government works, in particular how the *constitutional position* of the civil service has changed. These are:

- the responsibility which ministers exercise on behalf of their civil servants has been weakened;
- the anonymity of senior civil servants has been eroded;
- Civil Servants are now less permanent. Though it remains a relatively secure occupation, careers are now more vulnerable;
- the work of civil servants is more closely monitored than ever before;
- There is less emphasis on administrative *methods* and more on the *quality* of service provision.

STUDY GUIDE

---

### Revision Hints

It is vital for any study of the civil service for students to grasp fully the nature of all the reforms which have taken place, certainly since 1979. It is also useful to have a few notes in the experience of the Fulton Report. Notes should include the reasons which lay behind the reforms, the nature of those reforms and their results. It is especially important to note the political background to reform and to bring the issue right up to date with recent Labour proposals. Reform is a continuing process so that students should constantly update to take account of new developments.

Reforms have tended to fall into fairly clearly defined phases so that it is logical to set out notes in this way. A good scheme would use the following headings: 1968–70, 1979–90, 1990–97, 1997 onwards with the most recent developments.

---

### Exam Hints

Many examination questions require a full description of the reforms. It is not necessary to go back as far as Northcote-Trevelyan in the last century and the Fulton reforms could safely be covered very briefly. Fulton should be mentioned in exam answers only as an illustration of what was seen as wrong with the civil service before 1970 and how early reforms basically failed. Students must, however, be prepared to describe thoroughly the post 1979 reforms. Description, however, is not enough. Some analysis will usually be required. Answers should therefore describe the extent and the significance of the reforms. Students should be prepared to give an overview of how the reforms have changed the nature of central government in Britain and how they have affected the constitutional and political status of civil servants.

---

### Practice Questions

1   "Civil Service reform since 1979 has been so radical that the nature of government in Britain has been fundamentally changed." Discuss
2   Why did the Conservatives wish to reform the civil service after 1979? To what extent has Labour followed the Conservatives' principles of reform and to what extent have they departed from them?

# 5

# THE MACHINERY OF CENTRAL GOVERNMENT

## *Introduction*

THE TRADITIONAL STRUCTURE of the British civil service has been based on the system whereby each official saw himself as a member of a government department. Membership meant a complete loyalty to the work of that department and to the political ministers who led it at any given time. In many cases it also meant that a civil servant would spend all or most of their career in one single department. There was little sense of serving the government *as a whole*. Indeed, until the 1980s, only a handful of officials served government at the centre, and many of these civil servants attached to the Cabinet Office, were only seconded from their normal departmental homes. They might spend a few years in Downing Street, where the Cabinet Office is sited, and then return to their own departmental careers. Only the Cabinet Secretary, Britian's most senior civil servant, and a small group of permanent staff could be said to form a central bureaucracy.

When one considers that the British system of government has a strong reputation for a concentration of power at its centre – that is with the prime minister and the cabinet – it is remarkable to see that such a tiny proportion of the civil service served these centralised functions. It could be argued that the Treasury is a central body with its key role of providing financial discipline and distributing to various public services. It is also true that every government must report constantly on its financial dealings to the Treasury and, from time to time, go cap in hand for its support. But the Treasury operates more as a *regulatory* body at the centre, rather than a policy making institution. Apart from economic and financial decision-making, the Treasury is not directly involved in the broad sweep of government policies except as a safeguard against excessive spending levels.

During the 1980s commentators on the civil service and a number of politicians, led notably by prime minister Thatcher, became concerned by this apparent vacuum. The machinery of central government was expected to provide decisive leadership, but was almost totally lacking in independent sources of political advice. It was, therefore, at this time that a steady growth in the central bureaucracy emerged. Before we consider this development, we must review the nature of British government at the centre, as it stands at the beginning of the twenty-first century.

# THE CABINET SYSTEM

## THE CABINET

The twenty or so senior ministers, selected by the prime minister to direct the work of government and give it political direction, form the cabinet. This is the centre of political power in Britain. Every key decision, with the exception of the annual government Budget, must be approved by the cabinet. It is not a deliberative body on the whole and is becoming less so as time passes. It is unusual for cabinet members to spend their time together giving profound consideration to a variety of policy options. Yet the cabinet *is* expected to process every important decision and policy and does have the opportunity to veto parts of the government programme and to change its priorities.

Each minister is invited to review proposals presented by the prime minister himself or by their cabinet colleagues who head other departments. They are aided in this process by their senior officials who will suggest to them what might be an appropriate response. In other words, cabinet members consider policies from the point of view of *their own* department. It takes hard work and an act of will for a busy departmental minister to look at general government policy in a truly independent fashion. Every instinct of the minister and of his senior civil servants is either to say, 'this proposal has little to do with my department's work so I can ignore it and simply nod approval when it is brought before cabinet' ... or to say 'I can approve of those parts of the policy which do not adversely affect my department but I may object if parts of it may cause me some problems.' Ministers do not necessarily think, 'I fundamentally agree with this policy proposal, whether or not it affects my department. I can therefore actively support it.'

What has been lacking in this system is a mechanism whereby civil servants can handle the presentation of policies to cabinet *as a whole*. This implies briefing ministers, not from the point of view of their own department's interests, but in consideration of how the nation's and the government's interests can be furthered. There were in other words, thousands of civil servants available to give advice to individual ministers, but few to advise the cabinet as a *collective* body.

### Cabinet Committees

The work of the cabinet has increasingly been delegated to sub groups of ministers known as cabinet committees. These came into existence in the early 1920s. Their role is to consider specific aspects of policy in some detail. Having reached their conclusions the committee may then announce a new policy if they are empowered to do so, or will recommend action to full cabinet. At each of its weekly meetings, much of the work of cabinet will be to approve, or occasionally refer back, proposals coming from committees.

As with full cabinet the committees need to be supported by relevant sections of the civil service. Each committee is shadowed by an *official committee* made up entirely of civil servants. The role of the official committee is to supply information, to present viable options and to give administrative support to the cabinet committee. Those civil servants who shadow cabinet committees and support them perform one of the most influential roles in the whole government structure. Ministers rely heavily on their advice and the full cabinet in turn tends to follow the lead given by one of its ministerial committees.

The number, functions and membership of cabinet committees is constantly changing so there exists no permanent establishment. However a list of some of the principal committees which existed in September 1999 is instructive as to their functions and scope:

| | | |
|---|---|---|
| **Economic Affairs** | **Environment** | **Crime Reduction** |
| **Local Government** | **Utility Regulation** | **Constitutional Reform** |
| **Better Government** | **Home and Social Affairs** | **Defence and Overseas** |
| **Legislation** | **Food Safety** | **Northern Ireland** |

This is not an exhaustive list. There were many other committees and sub-committees reflecting both long term and short term concerns. The total number of committees and sub-committees in the Autumn of 1999 was 31. This indicates the enormous degree of co-ordination work the Cabinet Office and the official committees must do.

The organisation of the cabinet and its committee system has not fundamentally changed in the second half of the twentieth century. However, when we turn to the Cabinet Office, the main supporting agency for the system, we can see dramatic changes taking place.

### The Cabinet Office

Up to the 1980s the Cabinet Office played a relatively limited role in the affairs of central government. Its head, the Cabinet Secretary, certainly did lend vital support to the prime minister, and cabinet relied heavily upon the Office for administrative support. But these were modest functions. In the last twenty years of the century, and in particular after Labour took over government in 1997, the role of the Cabinet Office was transformed. In 1998 it was amalgamated with the Office of Public Service, further widening its scope.

The clear statement of its aims, published in 1998, tells us the extent of its functions:

---

*To help the prime minister and ministers collectively to reach well informed and timely decisions on policy and its presentation, and to drive forward its implementation, together with their agenda for modernising government, for improving the quality, coherence and responsiveness of public services, and for promoting a strong and well managed civil service.*

(source: Cabinet Office 1998)

---

This 'mission statement' – for that is what it amounts to – is indeed a far cry from the small administrative body which played a large administrative role in the work of government before 1980.

To match its increased importance the Cabinet Office has sprouted an impressive collection of sections, task forces and other agencies which are directly or indirectly within its control. In late 1999 such bodies included:

**The Social Exclusion Unit**
**The Centre for Management and Policy Studies**
**The Performance and Innovation Unit**
**The Efficiency and Effectiveness Group**
**The Better Regulation Unit**
**The Women's Unit**
**Anti Drugs Co-ordination Unit**
**Committee on Standards in Public Life***
**Political Honours Scrutiny Committee***
**Security Commission***
*These operating independently of ministers

There are three ministers (the most senior of whom sits in the Cabinet) who provide political control for the Cabinet Office. These ministers are supported by a large group of senior civil servants. This senior establishment now ranks favourably, in terms of size and authority, with many of the traditional government departments. In addition the agencies of the Cabinet Office have introduced a major innovation into the machinery of government. Within the bodies described above, civil servants are required to share their functions with experts drawn from outside the civil service. Many individuals have been co-opted or temporarily transferred into Cabinet Office committees and advisory bodies to work alongside the permanent staff. In the past the functions of insiders (civil servants) and outsiders have tended to be clearly differentiated. This has preserved the neutrality of civil servants. The distinction, at least within the Cabinet Office, is being steadily eroded.

The functions of the new Cabinet Office can be summarised as follows:

- providing administrative support and organisation for the cabinet and its committees (the **Cabinet Secretariat** section);
- supporting the prime minister in his role as leader of the government;
- handling the presentation of government policy, ensuring collective responsibility and consistency among ministers;
- dealing with disputes which may arise among ministers;
- co-ordinating those policy areas which cut across different departments;
- managing the re-structuring and modernisation of the government machinery;
- controlling the recruitment and promotion of civil service staff;
- managing the drive for greater efficiency and effectiveness of government;
- identifying those areas of government which may be suitable for privatisation or partnership with the private sector.

A number of interpretations can be placed upon the radical development of the Cabinet Office under the Labour government of 1997 onwards. These include the following:

1  **An extension of prime ministerial power.**
   In the past, the prime minister has suffered from a lack of his own independent sources of policy and advice. Compared to departmental ministers his support system was always relatively modest. This is no longer the case. While it has been true (since its founding in the 1920s) that the Cabinet Office exercises considerable control over the cabinet system, its new expanded functions represent an important extension to the potential powers of the prime minister.

2  **An agent of 'Joined-Up Government'.**
   If the policy-making functions of government are indeed to become capable of cutting across departmental lines, as the *Modernising Government* initiative of 1998 suggests, there has to be a co-ordinating body which can help the process along and can co-ordinate the work of the various departments and agencies involved. The Cabinet Office has been beefed up to perform this task.

3  **Co-ordinator of the Presentation of Government Policy**
   The determination – some say obsession – with which the New Labour government of 1997 has pursued its aim of managing the public presentation of its policies, has necessitated the creation of an extensive machinery for controlling information. This role, largely in the hands of the prime minister's press office in the past, has now been strengthened and extended. The press officer, Alastair Campbell in the case of prime minister Tony Blair, remains the principal co-ordinator, but he now has at his disposal the whole communications establishment within the Cabinet Office. This is a formidable role and seems set to grow further in the new century.

## 4 Supervisor of the Civil Service and Its related Bodies

When Margaret Thatcher set up the Efficiency Unit within the Cabinet Office in 1979 she started a trend which has continued ever since. This is the transfer of responsibility for the running of the civil service from the Treasury to 10 Downing Street. The Cabinet Office continues to monitor efficiency and quality within the civil service, but has added the pursuit of several other goals such as modernisation (the *Modernising Public Services* Group), innovation (the *Performance and Innovation Unit*), better recruitment practices (the *Recruitment and Development of People Group*) and quality of service (the *Performance Management Group*). The prime minister's official position of 'Head of the Civil Service' has now become a genuine reality through his leadership of the Cabinet Office.

### *The Cabinet Secretary*

No picture of the Cabinet Office would be complete without consideration of the role of the Cabinet Secretary. The holder of this post is one of the most influential individuals in the political community. Apart form being Britain's most senior civil servant, he has the ear of the prime minister, is constantly consulted by him and has his finger firmly on the pulse of cabinet government. Some Cabinet Secretaries have reached such positions of influence that they have boasted more political power than all but the most senior of cabinet ministers. Yet for all this he is unelected, cannot be held accountable for this actions by parliament and owes his position almost completely to prime ministerial patronage. In short he is an *eminence grise*, a power behind the prime minister's throne. He is unknown to most members of the public, but is in charge of many of the key aspects of government.

The Liberal prime minister Lloyd George, who created the post in the 1920s, certainly intended him to be powerful. He also intended that he should act largely as the prime minister's personal servant. Lloyd George was interested in extending prime ministerial power and knew that he needed a lieutenant who would be free from most political pressures. By choosing a *civil service* post for this function he ensured that he would have such a man. Maurice Hankey, the first Cabinet Secretary, shaped the position in this light and it has remained so ever since.

Of course the influence of the Cabinet Secretary is never constant. It varies according to the personality of each prime minister and according to how the prime minister wishes to use him. Nevertheless there has been a steady trend towards the accumulation of power in his hands. To some extent, of course, the growing influence of the Cabinet Office as a whole has resulted in the increasing stature of its Chief. Thus the last four Cabinet Secretaries of the twentieth century – John Hunt, Robert Armstrong, Robin Butler and Richard Wilson (all knighted by tradition) have played a significant role in shaping British politics. Hunt (in Professor Peter Hennessy's view the most influential Cabinet Secretary of the

SIR RICHARD WILSON, CABINET SECRETARY

modern era) helped to prop up the constantly weak and sometimes tottering Labour governments of 1974–79, Armstrong and Butler helped to see through the great reforms of Thatcher and Major, and Wilson managed the dramatic transition from Conservative to New Labour style of government.

The question of precisely why a civil servant should enjoy so much political clout is not an easy matter to resolve. It is certainly true that he wields more power than the *official* functions he performs would suggest, but how does this come about? The short answer is that he carries with him the authority of the prime minister in everything he does. The longer answer is more complex. We can, however, distil the sources of his power down to the following factors:

- he enjoys the delegated authority of the prime minister;
- he can control the flow of information around the political community. This is in the form of the minutes of cabinet and cabinet committee meetings as well as the briefings which ministers receive from the Cabinet Office on matters of policy;
- he is often required to settle disputes between ministers outside the cabinet room;
- he and the prime minister co-operate on the way cabinet meetings are run and on how decision–making is delegated to cabinet committees;

- he ensures that cabinet meetings run as smoothly as possible and that policies and options are presented to cabinet in such a way as to avoid too much conflict or delay;
- it is often his role to make it known what the prime minister's view is on each issue. This is always likely to be highly influential. He does share this function today with the prime minister's personal advisers, but he is nevertheless a key figure in promoting the prime ministerial line.

These roles place the Cabinet Secretary at the very heart of the government machinery. When we speak of *civil service power*, it is to the Cabinet Secretary that we should look first.

# THE PRIME MINISTER'S OFFICE AND OTHER ADVISERS

The Cabinet Office exists, in the strictest sense, to serve the Cabinet *as a whole*, not just the prime minister. This is somewhat misleading in that many of its functions relate specifically to the prime minister as an individual. This was described in the previous section. Nevertheless, many Cabinet Office tasks relate to central government as a whole. It is therefore essential that the prime minister runs his own personal office, both for administrative and political reasons. As we shall see, he is served at 10 Downing Street by a variety of civil servants and private political advisers who work for him and him alone. The establishment can be divided for convenience into three sections – The Political Office, The Policy Unit and the team of personal advisers.

## THE POLITICAL OFFICE

As with most of the central government, the prime minister's office is undergoing change. In this case the reforms suggest a considerable strengthening of the assistance available to the prime minister. In particular the office of **Chief of Staff** has been created. This role, an import from the American White House, gives a focus for all the activities of the office and ensures that the prime minister's personal representative is always present. In addition a **Principal Private Secretary**, assisted by six **Private Secretaries**, gives the prime minister a small civil service department of his own. As an indication of the modern importance placed on presentation of policy, especially to the media, and communications in general, there is a team of 15 officials operating in this area, headed by the prime minister's **Chief Press Officer**. As we have seen above, Margaret Thatcher's chief press officer, Sir bernard Ingham, and Tony Blair's chief press secretary, Alastair Campbell, have become key elements in prime ministerial influence. Two MPs are also drafted into the office to assit the prime minister in his relations with the House of Commons. These are his **Parliamentary Private Secretaries**. They are not civil servants, but elected representatives.

The table below indicates the extensive nature of the modern prime minister's office:

| Table 8: *The Principal Members of the Prime Minister's Office* | | |
|---|---|---|
| TITLE | HOLDER AS AT JANUARY 1999 | GENERAL ROLE |
| Chief of Staff | Jonathan Powell | Co-ordinating the work of the office |
| Principal Private Secretary | Jeremy Heywood | Providing Policy Advice to the P.M. |
| Six private secretaries | Various | Policy advice on: Domestic Policy Foreign Affairs Parliamentary Affairs Home affairs Economic affairs |
| Parliamentary Private Secretaries | Bruce Grocot MP Ann Coffey MP | Managing the prime minister's parliamentary duties |
| Chief Press Secretary | Alastair Campbell | Providing Information for the Media |
| 8 Press Secretaries | Various | Assisting the Chief Press secretary |
| Strategic Communications Unit | 6 officials | Managing the flow of information around government |

SOURCE: CIVIL SERVICE YEARBOOK 1999

## THE PRIME MINISTER'S POLICY UNIT

It must be stressed from the outset that the Policy Unit is *not* staffed by civil servants. Nor is it required to respect the rules of political neutrality which constrain civil servants. However, it is relevant to any study of the civil service in the sense that, since its founding by prime minister Harold Wilson in 1974, it has replaced some of the functions which might, in the past, have been performed by civil servants. This is certainly true in terms of the prime minister specifically.

The Policy Unit is staffed by 'outsiders' who are temporarily seconded to government service. It is expected that they will ultimately return full time to their normal occupations. They bring to Downing Street a particular expertise which the prime minister may find useful in formulating *his own* policy initiatives. Departmental ministers have their own armies of civil servants to perform this task. The prime minister's office, as we have seen previously, remains relatively small. The Policy Unit is therefore an important addition. In 1999 it had 13 members, including its Head, David Miliband. They concern themselves with the whole range of government responsibilities. Solutions to old problems and new initiatives may be proposed, to be carried through by the prime minister and his own office.

### Special Advisers and Kitchen Cabinets

Peter Hennessy, one of the keenest observers of central government in Britain, has likened the modern prime minister's position to that of a medieval king. In what he describes as 'court politics', the prime minister is surrounded by courtiers and favourites, individuals who seek to advise him but are also hoping to find advancement and other favourable opportunities to enhance their status. When these groups become a recognisable unit they have been described as 'kitchen cabinets'. This phrase originated in the time of Harold Wilson when ideas and political tactics were discussed and planned late into the night in the kitchen of 10 Downing Street.

These less formal groups surrounding the prime minister may be made up of a variety of individuals. The chief press secretary is invariably one of them, but the others may be MPs, junior ministers, private party advisers and sometimes civil servants. Strictly speaking civil servants should not be involved in such political activity, but it is almost inevitable that some will be so close to the prime minister that they are regularly consulted. As long as their political involvement remains discreet there is unlikely to be any major disquiet. Margaret Thatcher certainly included three senior officials among her closest advisers. These were Charles Powell (mainly foreign policy), Bernard Ingham (information controller), and Peter Middleton (Economics). Together with her most trusted party colleagues such as Cecil Parkinson and Norman Tebbitt this group formed an influential establishment behind the scenes at Downing Street.

### CONCLUSIONS

The growth in the size and importance of the Cabinet office, together with the increasing significance of the Prime Minister's Office, presents both opportunities and challenges for the civil service. The two bodies provide ideal opportunities for younger, 'high flying' civil servants to advance their careers by experiencing life at the centre of government and by catching the eye of the prime minister himself. Indeed it has almost become an essential entry on the *curriculum vitae* of any aspiring official to have had a spell in Downing Street.

But it is also a threat to civil service influence. The growth in the use of advisers from outside government and the growing variety of special units, task forces or commissions, staffed again by non-civil service personnel, presents a challenge to the traditional pre-eminence of the established service. In particular, the fact that such 'outsiders' are not bound by the rules of conduct if the civil service – concerning political neutrality in particular – presents them with greater opportunities for genuine influence. It may well be that the days when the mandarins who headed the great departments of state were 'kings of the jungle' in Whitehall are numbered.

On the other hand civil servants continue to provide a service which outsiders cannot. This is the ability to provide ministers with entirely independent advice. They can say something which outside advisers cannot – that their role is untainted by the need to find political favour or to secure highly paid positions in public service. As long as they retain a high degree of job security and their conditions of service are generous, they can retain their status.

### Revision Hints

The growth in the political machinery at the centre of British government is a key issue at the end of the century. Students should understand clearly how central government is organised. The roles of the Prime Minister's Office and the Cabinet Office must be noted carefully. The growth in their importance should also be noted. Students should attempt to keep abreast of new developments as this is a changing area of modern government. The relationship between the cabinet system and the Cabinet Office itself should be understood clearly.

### Exam Hints

This is a relative new issue in studies of British government. Questions are likely to centre upon the extent to which the growth in the central government machinery represents an important extension in prime ministerial power. The material in this chapter should be added to more general work on the growth in the power of the prime minister, which is an extremely common examination question. Students should be in a position to make some assessment as to whether the changes described in the chapter will strengthen or weaken cabinet government.

### Practice Questions

1 Assess the importance of the Cabinet Office in the modern British system of government.
2 To what extent has the prime minister strengthened his power over the machinery of central government in Britain?

# 6

# THE CHANGING NATURE OF THE BRITISH STATE

## *Introduction*

IN CHAPTER 1 we saw what the nature of the state is in *general* terms, as well as how we can distinguish it from the term *government*. In the context of Britain itself the nature of the state could be defined in fairly clear terms. In addition the British state has remained remarkably stable and unchanging for over a century. It was a major feature of the state that the civil service stood very much at the centre of its organisation. But, at the end of the twentieth century, both the British constitution and the state that administers the constitution are in a state of flux. Two developments, which are interlinked, lie at the centre of these changes.

Firstly the actual *functions* of the state have altered. This has inevitably resulted in the second change, which is the creation of new kinds of institution, especially so-called **quangos**, in order to manage the new functions. It is convenient, and largely accurate, to place the starting point for these developments at the accession to power of Margaret Thatcher in 1979. Her determination – largely converted into concrete action – to reduce the role and size of the state provided the foundation for the transformation which can be seen twenty years later. We can now review the changes in some detail.

## ROLLING BACK THE FRONTIERS OF THE STATE

### TRANSFERRING FUNCTIONS

The neo-liberal, monetarist governments which were led by Margaret Thatcher and John Major between 1979–92 were committed to transferring many previous state functions to private enterprise or to the voluntary sector. The principal developments in this direction were as follows:

- Many large industries and state controlled enterprises were privatised. These included British Telecom, gas, electricity generation and supply, water, coal mining and the railways. These industries were merely some of the leading examples of a huge transfer of resources from the public to the private sector. Naturally enough, the civil servants who had formerly been involved in the development of ministerial policy in these sectors lost most of their functions.
- In many cases, rather than outright privatisation, services were subject to competitive tendering between public and private sectors. In such schemes, services would be open to competition between the state and private enterprise. Whoever could provide the most cost-effective service would be awarded a long term contract to supply them. This applied mainly to local government in such functions as waste collection, environmental services and building or road repairs. However, there was also more competition introduced in some central government responsibilities, notably the prison service, some medical services and maintenance of trunk roads.
- In some cases, where state-run enterprises enjoyed a legal monopoly and were therefore not subject to normal commercial competition, *liberalisation* took place. This is a process where private sector organisations are invited to compete for customers. Examples of such liberalisation were public transport services, mainly buses, some high value mail services and particularly in public broadcasting where there has been a veritable explosion in the private sector.
- It is not only private, profit-motivated enterprise which has benefited from the transfer of service. There have also been examples of functions being taken over by *voluntary* non-profit-making organisations. Housing is the principal illustration of this process. Housing Associations, funded through the Housing Corporation, have largely replaced local authorities in the provision of low-cost, subsidised rented accommodation. Similar developments have occurred in areas such as care of the elderly and medical research. Control over schools has also been transferred. Some have taken advantage of a scheme to become self-governing, freeing themselves from local authority control (so-called *opt-out schools*). Indeed *all* schools now operate *local management of schools*, a system which transfers most of the management to voluntary boards of governors instead of local government officers.

In all these cases the size of the state machine which used to control such services has been reduced in size. As we shall see below, this does not mean that the state is no longer involved. What it does imply, however, is that the state has a role which is both changed and reduced.

DISENGAGEMENT

In addition to these transfers of control from public to private sector there were some functions which the state simply stopped performing. Neo-liberal, monetarist economics which underpinned the policies of a succession of Conservative governments in the 1980s and 90s required that economic and financial markets should be allowed to operate free of government regulation. The state ceased to use *fiscal* policy (the control of taxation and government expenditure levels) to try to control the economy. Any temptation to interfere directly with inflation, wage levels or the performance of private companies was resisted. In the past governments have often taken specific actions to try to control economic developments, but after 1979 such interventions were very rare.

At the same time financial markets were de-regulated. Regulations and taxes which had, in the past, imposed close control over the activities of the City of London, were steadily removed. Banks and building societies, stockbrokers and credit companies were all allowed to operate more freely. By 1997 the Bank of England control over the level of interest rates was one of the few examples of state control over finance. It was left to the new Labour government to remove this final pillar and hand over interest rate regulation (and with it, effectively, the task of managing inflation) to an independent monetary policy committee.

PRIVATE FINANCE INITIATIVES (PFIS)

As something of a 'halfway house' to privatisation, the concept of the private finance initiative was developed in the 1990s. A PFI is effectively a collaboration between the private and public sector in the provision of major public investments. Whereas formerly the state had struggled to find large scale funds for major projects such as road and hospital building, school extensions, public transport projects and housing developments, there was now a new source of large scale finance.

The principle of private finance initiatives is that private sector bodies such as banks, property companies and investment groups should provide the funds for expensive capital projects. This relieves government of the problem of finding extensive funds from taxpayers' revenue at times when such funds may be scarce. In return, the private enterprises providing the finance are guaranteed a reasonable rate of return on their investment. In many cases, the private sector companies may also be given the responsibility for the maintenance of these developments, again in return for a fee. The role of the state in the provision of these projects is, therefore, substantially reduced.

When these changes were added to the process of *disengagement*, the privatisations and the liberalisations described above, we can see that Margaret Thatcher's promise to roll back the frontiers of the state had indeed been kept.

# THE GROWTH OF QUANGOS

## WHAT ARE QUANGOS?

The term 'quango' is a journalistic invention dating from the 1970s. It stands for **Q**uasi **A**utonomous **N**on **G**overnment **O**rganisation (originally the 'N' stood for National, but this has since been amended to 'non' in most analyses). In more recent years the term **Non departmental public body** (**NDPB**) has also been used, or even the shorter, less precise **extra governmental organisation** (**EGO**). In this book, however, we will continue to adopt the name **quango**.

The term 'quasi-autonomous' suggests that they are organisations which are *not* part of government, but which cannot be considered fully independent of government – hence the prefix 'quasi'. They are described as 'non government' partly because they are semi–independent and partly because their members are not strictly members of the government. Even the term 'organisation' is a little vague. In reality some quangos are little more than a small committee which meets only a few times a year. Others, by contrast, are very large permanent organisations with a full time staff, considerable powers and substantial financial support for their work. It is therefore rather difficult to sum them up. The best set of common features which can be identified are as follows:

- They are originally set up by a government department, usually directly by a minister and sometimes as a result of a cabinet committee recommendation.
- The members are appointed by government. Senior members of large quangos may be appointed directly by ministers, others are employed as a result of open advertisements, recommendations to ministers or through the Commissioner for Public Appointments. The Commissioner is a member of the Cabinet Office, who also monitors the way in which all appointments are made.
- Their functions, powers and method of operation are determined either by parliamentary legislation or by ministerial order under powers granted by parliament.
- They receive their funding through a government department.
- Once they have been established, and have been awarded their funds, they are expected to reach decisions free of political influence or direction by ministers and senior civil servants.
- Members of quangos vary from part time, unpaid volunteers, to highly paid, permanent officials. None of the members are civil servants (except as special advisers seconded to them) and they are not bound by civil service rules.

When we look beyond these common features, however, there is a wide variation in the nature and role of quangos.

## What Quangos Do

There is no simple answer to this question. The problem here is that there is no precise definition of what a quango actually is. Take, for example, those groups of parents and other governors who run schools which have opted out of local authority control and take their funding directly from central government instead. Are these quangos? Some say yes, others say they are not closely enough related to government. Similarly there are many National Health Service Trusts which manage groups of hospitals, doctors and other medical services. These trusts certainly have replaced central government functions and so there is more justification for describing them as quangos. Yet even here they are not always included.

Fortunately, as we are studying the civil service we need only include those quangos – the more important examples in essence – which have a bearing on the work of the civil service. In other words quangos which have replaced departmental civil service or those with which civil servants have to deal on a regular basis.

The main functions of different types of quango can be described as follows:

- allocating funds on behalf of government;
- advising government on policy and legislation;
- devising and enforcing regulations on a variety of activities and organisations;
- administering activities on behalf of government.

All quangos fall into one of the broad categories described above. Some fall into more than one. The table below offers a number of examples of each to illustrate their work:

| Table 9: *Quangos in Britain* ||
|---|---|
| TYPE OF QUANGO | EXAMPLES |
| Spending Agencies | Medical Research Council<br>National Lottery Boards<br>Sports Council<br>Arts Council<br>Regional Development Agencies<br>Housing Corporation |
| Advisory Bodies | Equal Opportunities Commission<br>Commission for Racial Equality<br>Environment Agency<br>Audit Commission<br>Law Commission |
| Regulatory Bodies | Monopolies and Mergers Commissions<br>Office of Fair Trading<br>Independent Broadcasting Authority |

| | |
|---|---|
| | Office of Telecommunications (OFTEL)<br>Office of Water (OFWAT)<br>Commission for Health Improvement (CHI)<br>Office for Standards in Education (OFSTED) |
| Administrative Bodies | NHS Trusts<br>Training and Enterprise Councils<br>Qualifications and Curriculum Authority |

These are some of the major quangos operating in Britain. They are only the tip of a huge iceberg. However, most quangos, whether large or small, fall into one of the categories in the table.

### Why Quangos are set up

Explanations for the growth of quangos since 1970 fall into two categories. Firstly there are indisputable reasons which are acknowledged by all involved. Secondly there is a theory that the real reasons for their growth lie in a more sinister process, which is denied in official circles, but has widespread support.

The **official** reasons for the existence of any quango are as follows:

- They may reduce the workload of ministers and civil servants.
- They provide opportunities for experts and interested parties to become involved in the governing process without them having to stand for election, be party members, or take up a career in the civil service.
- There may be an overwhelming reason why a particular task should be taken out of the political arena and instead be subject to objective, neutral consideration. This is especially true of regulatory bodies and the spending agencies. Although civil servants are constitutionally neutral, it may be felt that they are too much under the control of ministers.
- Many quangos have a regional role, so it is a means by which decision making can be taken closer to communities and involve local participation. This is true, for example, of Regional Development Agencies and the Training and Enterprise Councils.
- The membership and procedures of quangos can be more flexible than sections within government departments which are subject to civil service rules.
- Their work may not need to be full time and in many cases members may be unpaid so it can be a less expensive option than employing full time officials.

There are also a number of **theories** about why government often prefers to work through quangos than through executive agencies or the civil service proper. Among these are:

- It is a way in which the role of the state can be disguised. In an age when there is increasing suspicion of government power and influence, quangos may give the *appearance* of autonomy but are in truth examples of creeping growth in state regulation.

- They provide increased opportunities for patronage by ministers. As more posts fall into their control, their influence increases. In some cases, accusations have also been made that local party organisations actually exert complete control over appointments to quangos, so that their 'independence' is actually an illusion.
- Since quangos cannot be held directly accountable for their activities (indeed their meetings are often held without any public attendance and accounts of their processings are confidential) it can be seen as a way in which government can avoid democratic responsibility which might be obstructive or inconvenient.

### How many quangos are there?

Since we cannot define precisely what a quango is, it is impossible to establish how many exist. It was estimated in 1979 that there were about 2,100 quangos, and the incoming Conservative government was committed to reducing their number. This was to be done by amalgamations, by bringing functions back to government or by complete privatisation of their activities. There is little doubt that by 1992 there were fewer quangos, no matter how they were defined. However, it is impossible to say whether the claim that their number was reduced to below 1500 could be sustained.

The Labour government which came to power in 1997 was also committed to reducing quangos, but its early performance has been patchy. By the end of the century it seems likely that about 80 quangos will have been abolished but that there will also be 46 additional bodies which fit our definition. This is clearly not a dramatic development. It must also be pointed out that reducing the number of quangos does not necessarily mean that their importance has diminished. The signs are that quangos are here to stay and will continue to feature prominently in government. The focus of attention has moved away from numbers towards reforms of their operations.

### Why quangos are criticised

We have seen above that there are some features of quangos which appear to enhance fair and effective government. However, there are also strong criticisms about the way in which they have operated. The principal concerns have been as follows:

- They are not publicly accountable for their decisions, unlike government departments whose work comes under the constant scrutiny of parliament.
- There are questionable practices in the selection of their members. The process of membership selection is secretive and open to nepotism (granting of posts to personal or political friends and relatives), single party control in some regions, and to the practice whereby existing quango members choose their own successors. In this way the most appropriate participants might not be selected.

- Their deliberations are held in secret.
- There are too many of them, leading to duplication and, in some cases, over-regulation. The 'official' count suggests about 1,500 quangos in existence, but the Audit Commission, which monitors the performance of public sector bodies, suggests there may be nearly 6,000 of them.
- Many have been accused of waste, inefficiency and even corruption. For example, the **Nolan Committee**, which investigates standards in public life, has insisted that the quango state requires radical reforms.

## CURRENT POLICIES ON QUANGOS

A number of consultation documents concerning quangos have been published since 1997. The most important of these was *Opening Up Quangos*, published in late 1997. These have culminated in the White Paper, *Modernising Government*, unveiled in 1999. The details of reforms have still to be finalised, but the intentions of government are clear. These include:

- opening up appointments to a wider variety of people and ensuring that appointments are based on merit and expertise rather than political contacts;
- greater accountability, either through local authorities or through parliament;
- greater access for the public to meetings, reports and decision-making processes;
- wherever possible unnecessary quangos should be abolished and amalgamations should replace duplication of functions;
- quangos should be more responsive to public demands and opinions.

The reforms stop short of precise plans to have some important quangos directly elected and there is no guarantee that any of the proposed reforms will be more than a cosmetic exercise.

We should now investigate how the development of quangos plays a part in the broader question of how the nature of the British state has changed at the end of the century.

# THE NEW ENABLING STATE

As we have seen, the changes in the nature of the British state since about 1970 have been immense. We can summarise the main developments as follows:

- The transfer of many activities and enterprises from state to private ownership and control (privatisation).
- The subjecting of many state-run services to competition from the private sector.

- The introduction of new partnership systems between the private and public sectors.
- The growth in the importance of quangos at the expense of department-based civil service control.
- The greater requirements for public services to be responsive to the demands of the public and to ensure good value for money.
- The transfer of many state activities from central government department to executive agencies with semi-independent status.
- The disengagement of government from many aspects of economic and financial management.

This is indeed an impressive list, indicating fully how much has changed. The end result of these reforms has been to change radically the role of the state, so much so that commentators are suggesting it is no longer a *provider* state, but merely an *enabling* state. What so these terms mean?

## THE PROVIDER STATE

This is the state which was born at the end of the Second World War and which was designed to provide a wide range of services which most people could not, or preferred not to provide for themselves. The Welfare State, as much of it was known, provided education up to degree level, unemployment relief, subsidised housing, pensions and the like, personal and public health care, social services at family level and a range of other community benefits. It was also the state which was given the task of running a range of industries which accounted for, at its height, over 50% of the total industrial output of the country. The state organised and managed the building of roads, hospitals, schools, universities and colleges, managed environmental projects, built low-cost houses or flats and cared for the mentally ill and the elderly. It ran prisons, post offices, national parks, urban redevelopment schemes and public transport.

These and other services were effectively managed by ministers and civil servants based in Whitehall. This was a large army of three quarters of a million officials, all of whom owed their first allegiance to the government and its ministers. This was the provider state. But, as we have seen above, the state has relinquished many of its functions. As this process has occurred the nature of the civil service has altered too.

## THE ENABLING STATE

As the state no longer directly runs many of the services described above, we can legitimately ask, what is its modern role? Many have suggested its new role is best described as 'enabling'. This implies a number of tasks:

- In cases where services have been privatised, the role of the state is to see that the new private enterprises are being run in the public interest and not just for the sake of private profit. Thus we have seen bodies such as OFTEL (The Office for Water) and OFGAS (The Office for Gas) springing up to ensure this occurs. At their heads stand so-called 'regulators' who have the power to order privatised enterprises to reduce prices, improve quality or ensure greater safety.

- Some private enterprises, such as broadcasting, railways and the National Lottery have been contracted out to companies for a limited time period. The new state therefore must monitor their performance, decide whether contracts should be renewed when they have run out and set the terms of any new contracts which are agreed.

- The requirements of the Citizens' Charter demand that public services achieve targets of quality and reliability. Here again the state must monitor performance and report on necessary improvements to be made.

- In the past, all large-scale public projects were funded by the Treasury using taxpayers' money. The system of private finance initiative means that funding is shared by the private sector. Here the state must seek new sources of finance and arrange for contracts to be made with the private sector to ensure mutual benefits.

- If state enterprises, often run by local authorities, are forced to compete with private enterprise, the rules for this competition must be established and the future results monitored.

- Many administrative functions have been decentralised, their management being transferred to executive agencies, quangos and local authorities. Where this occurs the central state gives up direct 'hands on' control. This has occurred with the prison service, regional industrial development, urban renewal, the health service, education and policing among others. However, this does not imply a complete abandonment of responsibility. Standards must still be set, procedures established and controlled, funding arranged and appointments to the new bodies made. The state still has a substantial, if much changed, role to play.

- New initiatives are also in hand to establish more state controls over activities which have *always* been in the private sector, but which have been much less regulated in the past. Thus there is more control expected over health and safety at work, consumer protection, fair competition, working conditions and product quality control.

CONCLUSION

So the role of the state has been transformed in many areas, but not everywhere. Some state responsibilities have seen relatively little change. The Legal system retains most of its traditional administrative features, the Home Office still controls immigration, broad oversight of the activities of the police and the system of law enforcement in general. The Foreign and Diplomatic Services operate much as they have done for many decades, except where the impact of European integration is most felt. The Department of Defence, too, has been largely untouched except for the privatisation of some of its less sensitive services. But most parts of most government departments have been deeply affected. The roles, the procedures and the very *culture* of the state have been changed for ever.

Precisely how this affects the civil service itself is discussed further in Chapter 8.

STUDY GUIDE

All students of modern politics should understand fully what quangos are as they now pervade the whole system. A clear understanding of what they are, what they do and why they have become important should be constructed. It is also important to note the various arguments which suggest they may be an undesirable development, though this should be balanced by reasons which can be supported. The issue of whether quangos can be tolerated in a true democracy should also be identified.

More difficult, but equally important, is the process by which the British state has changed from a provider state to an enabling state. A clear set of notes describing the ways in which the roles of the state have changed should be constructed, especially since 1979. An extensive number of examples should be used to underpin these descriptions.

*Exam Hints*

Some questions deal with the issue of the growth in the importance of quangos directly. Answers should both describe the nature of quangos and give an analysis of their role. Criticisms of their operation should be balanced by the advantages of using quangos as opposed to overtly political bodies. There are less precise questions to be asked about the changing nature of the state. These may specifically refer to the descriptions of 'enabling' and 'providing' for the state, in which case a full understanding of these terms needs to be shown. Where the terms are not given, the student should introduce them in an answer as an explanation of how the state is changing.

*Practice Questions*

1 What criticisms have been levelled against the growth in the importance of quangos in Britain?
2 Assess the extent to which Britain now features an 'enabling' rather than a 'providing' state.
3 In what ways have the frontiers of the state really been 'rolled back' as Margaret Thatcher claimed they would be after 1979?

# 7

# CURRENT ISSUES FOR THE CIVIL SERVICE

## THE IMPACT OF EUROPE

### Roles

BRITAIN BECAME A member of the European Community (which has since become the European Union) on January 1st, 1973. Since then membership has created an increasingly large effect upon central government. Not surprisingly, therefore, the civil service has also had to adjust to the new environment. The principal changes have been as follows:

1 When making decisions, advising on policy and drafting legislation, civil servants now have the responsibility of ensuring that there will be no conflict with existing European legislation. Where such a conflict should arise it is clear that the European legislation takes precedence. Should errors be made and a conflict arise, a challenge to the British government may be mounted in the European Court of Justice. This may be at best expensive and embarrassing or, at worst create major problems within the government. Such policy areas as the environment, industrial relations, trade, agriculture, fisheries, transport, consumer protection and welfare rights may be subject to such conflicts. As a response to these problems every government department now employs specialists in European legislation to prevent conflict. Even so, all civil servants have been forced to consider the European dimension in everything they do.

2 The European Union has no means of implementing and enforcing its own laws and regulations. This is the responsibility of member governments. Civil Servants are, from time to time, called upon to develop ways of implementing the wishes of the European Commission and the Council of Ministers. If, for example, new agricultural subsidies are ordered in Brussels, the officials at the Agriculture Department must ensure that they are paid to the appropriate

recipients. Similarly, fresh regulations on consumer information required in the sale of goods must be enforced. The relevant authorities, be they local councils, tax authorities, police departments or the law courts themselves, must be mobilised for this purpose.

3   Representatives of British government, both ministers and civil servants, must often spend time in Europe negotiating with their counterparts from fellow countries. Indeed, whenever meetings of ministers (known as the Council of Ministers for each department) are due to take place, the issues are first discussed among civil servants from the different countries. This may involve tough negotiations as well as an understanding of the issues involved. Needless to say, a knowledge of European languages is essential for those who are involved. By the time the ministerial meeting takes place, the civil servants are expected to have resolved most of the areas of potential conflict, leaving their political bosses to discuss and settle a few outstanding issues. At this stage, the officials must also ensure that ministers are fully briefed with the relevant information.

So, the civil servants who become most closely involved in European Union affairs must take a fresh perspective on policy. Not only must they consider the interests and possible reactions of up to fourteen other countries, they must also forge links with European agencies and pressure groups which may be able to provide vital information in the interests of sound policy making.

### *Institutions*

The key institution for civil servants in Europe is the **Committee of Permanent Representatives**, whose role is to undertake the negotiations which are necessary before each meeting of the Council of Ministers. There are just over 40 British representatives on this committee (collectively known as **UKREP**). These officials are Britain's most permanent representatives in Europe.

The Ministry of Agriculture, Fisheries and Food (**MAFF**) has more to do with the EU than any other government department. It therefore maintains its own permanent establishment of civil servants in Europe. They must ensure both that European directives are implemented successfully in Britain and that the ministry has an informed input into new developments.

Finally the Cabinet Office itself has developed a European dimension. The **European Secretariat** provides a clearing house for all European issues, ensuring that all those who need to know about what is happening in Brussels are kept fully informed.

### *Eurocrats*

The basic structure of the European Commission, which is the European Union's own bureaucracy, is described in the next chapter. Although British civil servants are expected to put aside their *national* allegiance when they work for the EU, very much in the same way as they are required to be *politically* neutral, they can be trained within the United Kingdom. About thirty applicants for European service are recruited on a 'fast stream' programme, with the expectations that they will rise quickly through the service and arrive in Brussels ready for a senior position. They operate first in the Cabinet Office, involving themselves exclusively in European affairs. They then transfer to one of the government departments, again dealing mainly with European policy, before going to Brussels. Once there they are commonly referred to as 'Eurocrats'. Their perspective must change completely, but in return they find themselves at the centre of a decision-making process which affects a community of hundreds of millions of inhabitants.

## DEVOLUTION AND THE CIVIL SERVICE

The transfer of governmental powers to Scotland and Wales in 1999, and the prospective establishment of devolved government to Northern Ireland may seem, at first sight, to have involved a major upheaval in the civil service. However, in practice, the change has proved relatively simple.

It has to be remembered that there have long been separate civil service departments for the three national regions. These offices already controlled much of the development, expenditure, and implementation of policy separately from Whitehall in such areas as health, education, transport, industrial development, planning and agriculture. It therefore became a fairly easy matter to transfer these bodies into the control of the new elected executives who took power.

Of course the civil servants involved (although some already worked in Cardiff or Edinburgh), have to adjust to the fact that they now work with different political masters. They must also accept that their work will be scrutinised by the new Scottish parliament or Welsh assembly rather than Westminister. But the principles remain the same, as does their constitutional status.

There are four principal ways in which the work of those civil servants who are transferring to devolved administrations may be affected:

- Their perspective will change from a British outlook to a *Scottish, Welsh* or *Northern Irish* one. In partial terms this suggests that they do not have to consider how policies impact upon Britain as a whole, but only upon the region in which they operate. For example, arrangements designed to benefit Welsh farmers might affect the general British market for their produce. On a British level, therefore, the whole picture would have to be considered. In Wales, by contrast, only the interests of Welsh farmers need be considered. Similarly, the thorny question of whether Scottish university students should pay the same £1000 fee contribution as their English counterparts, became a purely Scottish issue after July 1999. Civil Servants, when they advise politicians, are therefore free to consider a narrower range of consequences.

- There is a possibility in Scotland (and potentially in Northern Ireland), that the regulations concerning the activities of civil servants could be changed in the future. Since the Scottish parliament has legislative powers (the Welsh Assembly does not) it is able to make further reforms. Issues such as the anonymity or accountability of civil servants may certainly be re-considered by devolved assemblies.

- The financial arrangements for devolution are that in the main, Scotland, Wales and possibly in the future, Northern Ireland, will rely upon a block grant awarded by the British government and approved by parliament in London. Civil servants in the national regions will therefore no longer be involved in overall public expenditure planning. The most senior of them might, however, become heavily involved in negotiations on the size of the grant between London, Cardiff, Edinburgh or Belfast. Ministers will make final decisions, but the battle lines will be drawn up by their civil servants.

- Civil servants who are involved with drafting legislation or administrative regulations will face a doubly difficult task in the regions. Not only will they have to consider whether they are likely to conflict with European law, they will also have to review *British* law and avoid cutting across its constraints. It is a basic principle of devolution that, if there is a conflict between British law and proposed laws in Scotland (new laws cannot be made in Wales), the former shall prevail.

All this suggests that the new Welsh and Scottish civil servants may find their role more complex than in the days when power was concentrated in London.

# THE HUMAN RIGHTS ACT AND FREEDOM OF INFORMATION

## HUMAN RIGHTS

From the year 2000 onwards, civil servants will have further consideration to include in their deliberations and in their advice to ministers. This is the imposition of the Human Rights Act. The Act is, in fact, the incorporation of the European Convention on Human Rights into British law. Any executive action (i.e. decision), regulation or law, may be challenged in the British courts if it contravenes the Act. In essence the grounds for a challenge are that a basic human right has been abused. These may be straight forward questions of the right to free expression, free movement, association and thought or worship. Less clearly it deals with such matters as whether there has been discrimination against a minority, or whether an individual has not received fair and equal treatment. In these areas there may be a considerable degree of uncertainty until the judges have had their say.

In the past, of course, the European Court of Human Rights has been able to hear challenges to British law and administration, but these have been relatively rare (less than 100 since the 1960s) and were never binding on British government. It is also true that decisions or procedures have long been open to challenge in British courts under the principle of *judicial review*. Judicial Review has grown in importance considerably since the 1970s when it became popular. It became so significant that in 1987 the Cabinet Office issued civil servants with a document entitled *The Judge Over Your Shoulder*. This was a warning and a guide. It made civil servants aware of the fact that their decisions might be increasingly challengeable in the courts and gave guidance as to how they could safeguard themselves against such threats.

The typical cases which have been subject to judicial review are:

- where a minister or one of his officials has acted beyond his legal powers (so-called ultra vires cases);
- when proper procedures have not been followed so that an individual or organisation has suffered some sort of loss or disadvantage;
- where a decision or procedure discriminates against individuals or groups.

Although most judicial reviews are unsuccessful, civil servants have, nevertheless, grown used to trying to ensure that they are operating lawfully. Legal cases are expensive to defend and, if the government loses, can involve further expense, delay and embarrassment for the civil servant's department. The Human Rights Act will be a greater challenge, especially as cases under the Act are likely to attract considerable publicity, some of it adverse to government. However, there is every indication that civil servants are prepared for the additional constraints.

### *The Freedom of Information Act*

This Act, scheduled to become law in 2000, will have a marked effect on the so-called 'culture of secrecy' which pervades the British system of government, the civil service in particular. Before the Act it was possible to retain control over information held within central government. The general public and the media had no right to see any documents, reports or discussion papers used to make governmental decisions. Even parliament and its select committees were limited in their ability to look inside the civil service's files. Civil Servants have therefore enjoyed the security of knowing that a shroud of secrecy could be pulled over their work. Embarrassing information could be buried, unfavourable reports suppressed and, above all, their own anonymity safeguarded.

The new Act, though unlikely to be as powerful as its supporters hoped, will provide a further discipline upon the civil service. Where matters of national security are concerned, it will be possible to maintain secrecy. This will not be so where the general administration of government is concerned. In a wide range of areas it will become possible to see how decisions have been reached, to view the information upon which decisions were based and to see the differing views which were available. Civil servants will need to ensure that they and their ministers have followed procedures and can fully justify their decisions and policies. Although they may protect the national interest by keeping some documents secret, they will find it more difficult to protect themselves from charges of poor administration.

The indications, just as the new measure is about to be enacted, are that it will not be as strong as the rules operating in such democracies as the USA, France and Sweden. There will still be scope for information to be withheld. It will largely be the role of civil servants to decide what they can reveal and what they can legally keep confidential. The onus is likely to be on applicants for information to prove that it is in the public interest to publish, so officials may retain a strong position in this field.

## NEW LABOUR REFORMS

Despite two decades of almost continuous change, the civil service faces yet more reform from a government which is determined to modernise British administration. We have already seen how the Cabinet Office has been strengthened and extended. Also the idea of 'joined-up government', with its need for new institutions both inside and outside the civil service, to co-ordinate policy making. Tony Blair has committed his government to the creation of more executive agencies, to more privatisation where it is appropriate and to more partnerships between the private sector and government. So is there still more to come?

Certainly it is evident from the White Paper *Modernising Government* of March 1999 that there is. The principle areas for further change are:

- an even more flexible approach to recruitment, training and recruitment of staff;
- applying ways of making the civil service more responsive to public needs;
- greater opportunities for movement of officials between departments;
- greater financial and career incentives for officials who can improve their performance.

Little is new here. The proposed reforms represent a continuum dating right back to the Rayner reforms of the early 1980s. The underlying principle remains that if a service can be best provided by the private sector it should be so. Where it cannot, the public sector (largely civil servants, whether in executive agencies or not) must operate as closely as possible to the way the private sector *would* operate if it were responsible for the service.

What is new at the end of the century is the process of breaking down barriers between different parts of government. Increasingly policy development and implementation is no longer reserved to individual government departments, but is being transferred to bodies which can co-ordinate work across the whole range.

There is a further speculative discussion on how the civil service is likely to develop in Chapter 8.

It is unlikely that students would be asked about the issues discussed in this chapter as they relate *specifically* to the civil service. Nevertheless the general issues of Britain's relationship with the European Union, the Freedom of Information Act, the Human Rights Act and New Labour's modernisation plans will be common subjects in examination questions. Where this occurs students will need to be prepared to describe *all* the implications of the developments, not just how they relate to the civil service. Therefore, the material in the chapter is best added to notes on these topics which may deal with the rest of the political system. It is often the case that students, when asked to discuss the impact of Europe, for example, neglect the civil service. This omission should not be made. When such questions as this arise:

- Discuss the impact of membership of the European Union upon British government.
  or
- What impact is a Freedom of Information Act likely to have on the British political system?

Students should be prepared to include the civil service in their answers. This chapter provides material for such responses and therefore should be carefully noted.

# 8

## CONCLUSIONS

## SOME COMPARISONS

OUR UNDERSTANDING OF any institution can be deepened by comparisons with its counterpart in an alternative political system. We will, therefore, take a brief look at civil service practices in four different environments before reaching final conclusions.

### *France*

It is useful to compare the British civil service with that of France as it is possibly the most meaningful contrast we can find in the democratic world. There are important similarities between the two, but also instructive differences. It is also interesting to note that the French are moving towards the British system in some areas, while in others there are aspects of French administration which seem to be influencing British reforms. In other words, both systems would seem to have much to commend them and some combination of their best features might be effective.

We should begin with similarities. These are:

- The French service is a *career service*. For those who want it, there is a clear progression throughout the service to the highest positions. Most senior officials have spent all or most of their past career in the civil service.
- Entry to the service is based on merit, through examination success and is open to all who meet the requirements for entry.
- Civil Servants are expected to be neutral. This does have a different meaning in France, as we shall see below, but it is true that there is a strict code whereby French civil servants are bound to deal with all citizens equally, irrespective of political allegiance.
- French and British civil servants enjoy a similar degree of security. It is very difficult to remove either except for misconduct.

We can now survey the key differences. We will see that these are more extensive than the similarities.

- Senior civil servants, who are due to enter what is known as the **grand corps** of the service (the equivalent of the British senior civil service – both comprising about 3,000 members) have nearly all graduated from specific 'schools' specially for civil servants. These are the **École Nationale d'Administration and the École Polytechnique**. These are effectively postgraduate schools for the intellectual and technical élites for each generation. Not all graduates from the *écoles* enter the civil service – it is a qualification which is respected in the private sector – but it is a vital part of becoming a senior official. There is no near equivalent in Britain. The only similarity lies in the declining tendency for graduates of Oxford and Cambridge to be favoured in recruitment and promotion. The difference is that entry to the French *écoles* has always been based on merit, while this cannot be said for Oxbridge. It is also true, of course, that the *écoles* are designed *specifically* for French administration.
- There is in France a greater tendency for civil servants to transfer freely in and out of the service. Political neutrality is less strictly imposed, so it is common for civil servants to leave the service and become party politicians. They can also transfer back into the services at the end of a political career. To illustrate this, all Presidents, with only two exceptions – de Gaulle and Mitterand – since 1958 have been former senior civil servants. 15 of France's 18 prime ministers in the same period have similar backgrounds and 50% of all ministers. This is simply impossible in Britain. A few senior politicians have been junior civil servants in the past, but there is no modern incidence of direct transfer from the senior civil service into high politics. In France there is also a tendency for frequent transfers in and out of private enterprise (i.e. industrial or commercial management and banking), a process known as *pantouflage*. This has the effect of creating a civil service with a much wider variety of experience in direct contrast to Britain where civil servants rarely have any experience outside the service.
- Although the French state is very centralised, more so even than Britain, there is a strong provincial system that needs to be controlled. In order to achieve this the French civil service is divided into 96 regions, or *départments*, each one under the control of a Préfet (Prefect) who is effectively a local governor. The Prefect is a senior civil servant with wide powers in his own region and a large administrative set-up to help him. The British civil service has recently opened 12 regional offices, but this is on a tiny scale compared to France.
- The French definition of 'civil servant' is wider than in Britain. In particular, teachers are civil servants and are thus subject to a strict code of conduct. This means that there are over 2 million civil servants in France, though this figure is somewhat misleading owing to the wider definition of the term used there. However, it does mean that senior officials have considerably wider jurisdiction.

- There is no doubt that French civil servants enjoy higher social status than their British counterparts. This is a legacy of the Napoleonic age when the basis of today's service was laid down. This is partly the result of the greater acceptance which French citizens have of the power of the state. It is also caused by an understanding that civil servants, especially senior ones, have achieved their position on merit. They form part of an intellectual élite which is much respected.
- It is part of the tradition of the French civil service that they serve the state, as a permanent institution, rather than merely the government of the day and its ministers. Whereas British officials are required to faithfully serve their minister, their French equivalent can be more independent-minded and offer their own version of the national interest.
- There are about 200 senior civil servants in France who are allowed to have an openly political bias. These form what are known as ministerial *cabinets*, groups of about five officials who are chosen directly by each minister and who give him political advice. These are the equivalent of private advisers to British ministers, but are still classed as civil servants.

The French are interested in the reforms which have been made in Britain since 1979. They have largely followed the requirement that civil servants should pay more attention to the needs and demands of the public. There is also much admiration for the way in which improved performance evaluation has been introduced. In the opposite direction it is clear that British administrative practices are moving closer to those of France. There is now in Britain a looser distinction between 'political' and 'administrative' roles and a much more flexible approach towards recruitment and the career structure in general. Finally, and perhaps most significantly, more attention is being paid to the sheer quality of British civil servants. The French *école* has guaranteed high ability and specific training and there is now a determined effort in Britain to produce a similarly well qualified and educated administrative élite.

## The USA

Although the American political system is very different from those of France and Britain – it is federal in nature and has a much weaker party system – its civil service displays a number of similar features. Entry is by examinations which are open to all so that recruitment is on merit. There is a strict code of ethics, last updated in the *Civil Service Reform* and *Ethics in Government* Acts of 1978. It is also divided into distinct levels and contains an elite corps known as the *Senior Executive Service*. However, like France, there are a number of crucial differences which put the British experience in greater focus. The main features are:

- The distinction between a 'politician' and an 'administrator' scarcely exists in the United States federal system. The political heads of government agencies (the term 'ministry' is not used in the USA) may be drawn from any background. Indeed, the Constitution forbids them to be members of Congress while they hold government office. In effect the President is free to choose his political lieutenants however he wishes. Many, but not all, may be of the same political party as him, and many have no known political allegiance. it is therefore difficult to distinguish between a senior administrator and a politician.

- A very large number of posts in the American civil service fall under the patronage of the President. There are about 2,500 posts which he appoints and which are therefore non-permanent. There are another 600 senior positions which fall under presidential control, but which require the approval of Congress (the so-called 'advice and consent' principal). This leaves about 5,000 senior civil service posts which are permanent and are held strictly on merit, by non political appointees. Thus, the senior levels of the Administration are under considerable political control.

- Because of this political control, there is less requirement for a strict code of political neutrality. Whether or not a senior official shall hold office depends on the approval of the President. They are not bound in the same way to set rules.

- Senior Civil Servants owe their allegiance very much to the Administration of the day and this means effectively to the President himself. By serving the President, they are effectively serving the state. The position for British or French officials is certainly less clear.

- American civil servants have much closer links with the wide variety of pressure and interest groups which flourish in the USA and wield considerable influence. These links are actively encouraged as they are seen as an indication of good, responsive government. There are also, however, fears that too close a relationship results in what is known as 'agency capture', where the aims of an agency and those of a pressure group become the same. This creates 'iron triangles' – policy communities which cannot be penetrated and exercise excessive influence.

It must be stressed that although the American civil service is the product of a unique political system, there may be some lessons to be learned. Certainly the greater 'openness' of the administration to influence from an intensely pluralist political system could be admired. The British and French trust toward greater responsiveness could learn much from the United States. There are also dangers in this process, as are described above. The high level of political patronage which prevails in the USA is likely to be resisted in Europe. It is not part of our tradition and is treated with great suspicion. There is still in Britain and France a strong sense that a civil service independent of political pressures is healthy and safeguards the quality of policy advice.

### *The European Commission (of the European Union)*

The civil servants who administer the European Union are members of the Commission, which is situated in Brussels. The first thing to note is that it is much smaller than one might expect. There are about 16,000 officials – much smaller than most British or French ministries. The reason for this is that the majority of the implementation and administration of EU policies is carried out by member governments. The role of the Commission is therefore limited. It also has to be stressed that the political environment it operates within is completely different to those of individual states. The main features of the Commission are:

- It is divided into 17 sections, each one with its own set of functions such as finance, environment, transport and industry. Each section is headed by a Commissioner, normally an ex-politician, who reports to the European parliament. The overall head of the Commission is the 'President' of the Commission. His appointment and those of his colleagues are in the hands of the Council of Europe (a gathering of heads of government from all member states) or the Council of Ministers (a similar gathering of functional ministers).

- Both the commissioners and all civil servants are drawn from member states in rough proportion to the population of those countries.

- On becoming a European civil servant an individual is expected to abandon both their allegiance to any political *movement* and to their *national* origin. In short they should become politically neutral and stateless.

- They owe their loyalty to the European Union alone, as a *concept* (the European ideal of a single economic union) and *institution*. This mean that they are committed to implementing all the European Union Treaties and Directives which are in existence and should pursue the broad aims of the Union.

- Because the EU has no permanent government, operating instead through regular meetings of national ministers, European Commisssion civil servants are more involved in the process of developing and drafting policy. By the time the council of ministers considers new legislation nearly all the work has been done by civil servants.

- Although European Commission civil servants are responsible for the implementation and enforcement of policies, they must rely on their counterparts within each member state to ensure that action is taken. This may prove to be both a relief and source of frustration to them.

It is inappropriate to draw meaningful comparisons between the European system and those of individual states. The EU does not conform to most governmental principles. However, it is of interest to note that these civil servants play a considerably greater role in policy making than their British, French and American colleagues. At the same time they are much less politically accountable than others. It is this contrast – between greater power and less accountability – which forms the basis of the so-called 'democratic deficit' in Europe.

## Communist Systems

We need spend little time on this subject as communist systems are now rare in the world. China is the only major example of such a bureaucracy and even this exists within an economic system which is gradually moving towards capitalism. However, there is some value in making comparisons. The first thing to note is that the bureaucracies (the term civil service is less appropriate in these cases) fell under the complete control of a single ruling party. They were, therefore, *totally* political in a sense. Their purpose was not to serve the state in a *neutral* manner, but to serve the interests of the ruling party – the communist party of course. it is true that the ruling party always *claimed* to represent the interests of the state, but this was not a view shared by all. These bureaucracies were enormously powerful. Since, in communist systems, virtually all production and distribution of goods and services, employment and welfare are in the hands of the state, the bureaucrats commanded vast amounts of resources. If it is true that 'power corrupts', these systems were the most vulnerable to corruption in history.

There was a tendency for corruption in communist states. This was partly the result of economic shortages. It is to be expected that, when such deprivations exist, those in charge of the distribution of goods and services – the bureaucracy – should seek and find opportunities to accept bribes in return for favours. There was also political corruption. Recruitment and promotion would typically be reserved to party members, their relatives and friends. Merit was only one of many factors in determining who should rise to the top. This tended to promote inefficiency and a lack of any incentive to improve administration. There were many other problems, but as we have said, there is little need to detail them as these situations have all but disappeared. They do, however, serve as a warning to any state which may be heading towards single-party domination.

## Other Non-Democratic Systems

It is not the intention here to define what is, and what is not, a democracy. However, it is clear that there are many modern states which cannot be considered, in any commonly held sense of the word, to be democratic. What does the typical civil service look like in such state? By definition, of course, we must be careful about generalising. There are many different kinds of state which can be described as non-democratic. Nevertheless a few generalisations can usefully be made:

- Many countries which are former colonies have civil service systems similar to those of their former political governors. This is certainly true in many former British and French colonies in Africa and the Caribbean.
- In many cases the civil service is effectively running the country. This may be because there is so much instability that political government scarcely exists. It may also be true that rulers come and depart so frequently that only the civil service can ensure continuity.

- Legal and political control of the civil service tends to be weak. This means that there is a tendency towards corruption, inefficiency and nepotism.
- Many non-democratic states are effectively controlled by an élite group comprised of military leaders, businessmen and financiers. It is often the case that leading members of the civil service become part of this group, and therefore serve the élite group rather than the state as a whole.
- In countries where there are severe tribal, ethnic and religious divisions, control over appointments to the civil service is usually in the hands of dominant groups. This means that minorities, which may be sizeable, are often excluded from public service, resulting in discriminatory practices on a large scale. Indeed, it is often the cause of civil strife when the civil service does not deal with people in an even-handed way.

The picture is not, however, as bleak as it might seem. In some cases it is civil servants who are all that stands between order and chaos. There are also examples of civil service systems which have managed to retain some features of strong public service and fair treatment for all. In the worst cases, however, corrupt and inefficient civil administrations are adding to, not ameliorating, the country's problems.

The typically poor performance of civil services in communist states and other non-democracies indicates how vital democratic controls can be. Democracy will never eliminate all faults, but it is certainly true that the likelihood of corruption, wastefulness, discrimination and nepotism is severely reduced.

A typology of civil service is shown in the table below:

| Table 10: *A Typology of Civil Services* | | | | | |
|---|---|---|---|---|---|
| EXAMPLE | NEUTRALITY | PUBLIC ACCOUNTABLILITY | CORRUPTION | ENTRY | FAIRNESS |
| U.K | High | Declining | Rare | On Merit | Even-handed decisions |
| USA | Limited | Moderate | Low | Partly merit, partly political | Very even-handed |
| France | Limited | Fairly high | Low | On merit | Even-handed |
| EU | High | High | Some, not common | On merit | Even-handed |
| Communist | Must be communist | Low | common | By party alliegiance | Favours party members |
| Non-democracies | Limited | Low | High | Often according to social group | Often favours some groups above others |

# THE FUTURE OF THE BRITISH CIVIL SERVICE

In this book we have considered the main features of the British civil service. We have also reviewed the radical reforms which have taken place over the last twenty years of the 20th century. When we add these developments to the fundamental changes which are taking place in the nature of the British state and draw some contrasts with the experience of other political systems, we may be in a better position to consider the future.

## CIVIL SERVANTS IN THE ENABLING STATE

When Sir Robin Ibbs unveiled his 'Next Steps' programme, transferring civil service functions to executive agencies, he suggested that there could be as few as 20,000 civil servants in the traditional sense of the word. The other 400,000 or so would have lost their posts owing to privatisation, would be working in his semi-independent agencies, or would have transferred their work to one of the many advisory, regulatory and administrative bodies collectively known as quangos.

Instead there will be many servants of the state who will work within a variety of different institutions. They will have their own recruitment and promotion procedures, codes of practice, incentive schemes and internal management structure. Whether we will still call them 'civil servants' matters little. The importance of these developments lies in the fact that there will no longer be a unified civil service, the basis of which was established so long ago, in 1854.

There will still, of course, be traditional civil servants. That is officials whose role is to develop policy and advise ministers on its implementation. Whether or not there will be the 20,000 of Ibbs' estimate, such civil servants will always be needed. How will their political environment change?

## FUTURE REFORMS

During 1999 Tony Blair set in motion a consultation process within Whitehall to map out the future of the civil service. The main areas of reform are likely to be:

- A more open policy of recruitment. This would involve much more lateral entry into senior positions (a policy which was flagged up when Ed Balls, a *political* adviser to Chancellor of the Exchequer Gordon Brown, was appointed Chief Economic Adviser to the Treasury, a *civil service* post, in October 1999). Attempts will also be made to recruit more women and members of ethnic minorities to make the service more socially representative.
- A scheme of incentives is likely to be introduced to make the service more effective. The use of targets has already been introduced in such services as

education, policing and health care. These are likely to be extended into the senior civil service positions which manage policy.

- There is bound to be more movement towards 'joined-up government'. There will be greater encouragement to break down even further the traditional barriers between government departments. Civil Servants will increasingly work with, and become members of, bodies which will adopt holistic, cross-cutting approches to policy making. This suggests a Civil Service perhaps less unified in name, but more unified in aim.
- There will be an increase in the use of systems to try to ensure that the civil service is more sensitive to the demands of the public.
- Continued emphasis will be placed upon the *presentation* of policy, not just its development and implementation. More civil servants than ever are likely to be engaged in this field.
- The strict barriers which used to exist between the neutral civil service and political advisers are likely to be increasingly broken down. We are likely to see more of the French practice whereby officials move more freely between an administrative and a political role.

This is indeed a far cry from the vision presented in the 'Yes Minister' TV series described earlier in this book. There is no doubt that the politicians are now firmly in control. Whether or not this means that Britain will have a more effective civil service remains to be seen. The final question does, however, remain. Are the democratic safeguards over the civil service strong enough? The traditional system whereby civil servants were made responsible to parliament through their ministers has all but disappeared. As yet there is little to replace it. Civil Servants may indeed become more sensitive to the needs of the public and more responsive to the wishes of their political masters, but this is not the same as democratic control.

STUDY 🄴 GUIDE

Students who are undertaking a course or part of a course on comparative politics should certainly familiarise themselves with the basis upon which the civil service systems of other countries work. Though most comparative material concentrates on such areas as the legislature, heads of government, constitutions and political parties, the differing role and political status of civil services is a useful source of comparison.

For those who are exclusively concerned with Britain, it is nonetheless useful to be able to quote from the experience of other countries. For example if issues such as political neutrality, civil service influence or politicisation are discussed it is good practice to draw from foreign examples. A knowledge of the key features of the British, French and other systems should therefore be developed for appropriate use.

Where future developments are concerned, students should certainly note all current proposals. This concluding chapter suggests a number of areas where change is most likely and can therefore act as a guide for future research.

As we have suggested above, it is in the field of comparative government where much of the material in this chapter can prove useful. Students who need to answer comparative questions should be prepared to draw out the main distinction which exist between the British system of administration and one or two alternatives. France and the USA are commonly quoted for this purpose, but it would provide some originality if brief reference were made to the EU, to communist systems and non-demoncracies.

1  With reference to two or more political systems, discuss the ways in which bureaucrats may become politically influential.
2  In what ways can civil servants be made more politically accountable for their actions?

# GLOSSARY

**Armstrong Memorandum**   A document produced in 1985 by the Cabinet Secretary explaining the official version of the appropriate relationships between ministers and civil servants.

**Bureaucracy**   A term meaning literally 'rule by officials'. Used to describe any large formal organisation which exists for administrative purposes.

**Cabinet Office**   A central civil service department which gives administrative support to the cabinet and co-ordinates aspects of government policy for the prime minister, the cabinet and government as a whole.

**Citizens' Charter**   A series of commitments and targets for the performance of various public services. Established by John Major.

**Civil Service College**   A college which runs courses and conferences for civil servants as part of their training and development.

**Comprehensive Spending Review**   Established in 1998. It is a system for the long term planning of public expenditure.

**Ecole Nationale d'Administration**   A French postgraduate school which trains prospective civil servants in administrative and management skills.

**Ecole Polytechnique**   A French college for the training of specialist technical administrators.

**Efficiency Unit**   Set up by Margaret Thatcher in 1979 under the control of Sir Derek Rayner. Its role was to devise ways of making civil service operations more efficient.

**European Commission**   Effectively the civil service of the European Union

**Executive Agencies**   Set up in the 'Next Steps' report. They are semi independent agencies which carry out services formerly administered by civil service departments.

**Fast Stream**   A system for recruiting 'high flyers' to the civil service for rapid promotion to senior posts.

**Financial Management Initiative**   Devised by the Efficiency Unit in the early 1980s. A system for improved financial management within government departments.

**Freedom of Information Act**   Likely to come into force in the year 2000. It will require government to release a wide range of documents and information to parliament and the public.

**Fulton Report**   Presented in 1968 it proposed a number of civil service reforms. Largely unsuccessful in its implementation.

**Human Rights Act**   An act of parliament coming into force in 2000. It gives courts the power to reverse actions by ministers, civil servants and other bodies if they infringe human rights. The courts may also declare an act of parliament undesirable on the grounds of abuse of rights, but not strike it down.

**Joined-Up Government** Developed in the 1990s, mostly by the Labour Government after 1997. It is a method of dealing with policies across several government departments and agencies, rather than separately by individual departments.

**Lateral Entry** A system of recruiting senior officials from fields outside the civil service.

**Mandarin** A colloquial expression describing a senior civil servant. In common usage in political circles.

**Market Testing** A device whereby the performance of government and other state bodies is compared with the private sector to assess its efficiency.

**Next Steps** The name of a report presented by Sir Robin Ibbs in 1988. It proposed setting up executive agencies (see above).

**Northcote-Trevelyan Report** Written in 1854, the report established the principles of the civil service between 1970 and the 1980s.

**Permanent Secretary** The most senior civil servant, head of the Cabinet Office and principal civil service adviser to the prime minister and cabinet.

**Politicisation** A process whereby civil servants may lose their traditional neutrality either through partisan recruitment policies or by requiring officials to undertake political work.

**Quango** Stands for quasi-autonomous non government organisation. A body set up and funded by government but which acts in a non-political manner. Can be administrative, advisory or concerned with public spending.

**Scott Enquiry** In 1993 Sir Richard Scott produced a damning report on the way ministers and civil servants has secretly made policy on the sale of arms to Iraq, misleading parliament and the public in the process.

**Senior Civil Service** Members of the top five ranks of the civil service.

**Treasury** Effectively the Finance Ministry for British government. It controls taxation, public expenditure, finance and advises the government on economic policy.

**Vicar of Bray** A character in a song. He changed his sermons depending on which king was on the throne. Symbolic of the way civil servants can serve different governments equally well.

**Whitehall** The London street where many civil service departments are situated. It has become a general expression replacing the term 'civil service'.

# FURTHER READING & RESOURCES

## BOOKS

**Whitehall by Peter Hennessy Fontana, 1989**
This is for serious students only. It is a very long work on the modern civil service, full of anecdotes and references. Ideal for all, however, as a reference book.

**The Civil Service under the Conservatives 1979–1997 by David Richards. Sussex Academic Press, 1997**
The definitive work on reforms and developments during the period.

**The New Civil Service by Jonathan Tonge. Baseline Books, 1999**
Commendably concise, this small book gives an account of recent developments.

**British Government: The Central Executive Territory by Peter Madgwick. Philip Allan, 1991**
Places the civil service in its context. Describes the structure of central government and how the civil service fits into this structure. Very clear and concise.

## WEBSITES

Some useful internet sites for reference and factual information are:

**www.open.gov.uk**

The main government site with references to all main sources

**www.cabinet-office.gov.uk**

takes you through the central territory of British government

**www.civil-service.co.uk**

A huge amount of factual information and statistics

## JOURNALS

The two main journals for students of politics are **Politics Review and Talking Politics**. Back numbers are availiable. Some recent articles on the civil service have been:

**Labour and the Quango State. M. Flinders and M. Cole**
*Talking Politics.* Summer 1999. Vol.12. Number 1
**Tradition and Change in the Civil Service. J, Greenwood**
*Talking Politics.* Spring 1999. Vol.11. Number 3

**Whatever happened to the Scott Report? J. Adams and R. Pyper**
*Talking Politics*. Spring 1997. Vol.9. Number 3
**Evaluating the Quango State. T. Stott**
*Talking Politics*. Winter 1995–6. Vol.8 Number 2
**The Civil Service in the 90s. T. Butcher**
*Talking Politics*. Autumn 1995. Vol. 8. Number 1
**Quangos in British Politics. D. Wilson**
*Politics Review*. September 1996. Vol. 6. Number 1
**The Changing Civil Service. T. Butcher**
*Politics Review*. September 1995. Vol. 5. Number 1
**Individual Ministerial Responsibility. R. Pyper**
*Politics Review*. September 1994. Vol. 4. Number 1

# INDEX